For Grades
1&2

Parent/Teacher Edition

Write
on Target

Using Graphic Organizers
to Improve Writing Skills

Written By:
Yolande F. Grizinski, Ed.D.
Leslie Holzhauser-Peters, MS, CCC-SP

Show What You Know® Publishing

Published by:
Show What You Know® Publishing
A Division of Englefield & Associates, Inc.
P.O. Box 341348
6344 Nicholas Drive
Columbus, OH 43234-1348
(614) 764-1211
www.showwhatyouknowpublishing.com

Printed in the United States of America
05 04 03 02   20 19 18 17 16 15 14 13 12 11 10 9 8 7 6 5 4 3 2 1

ISBN   1-884183-93-X

About the Authors

Yolande F. Grizinski received a Bachelor's degree from Miami University, a Master's degree from Wright State University, and a Doctor of Education from the University of Cincinnati. She has worked in public education for 28 years as a curriculum consultant in the areas of language arts with a focus on writing assessment. She is currently the Assistant Superintendent of the Warren County Educational Service Center in Lebanon, Ohio.

Leslie Holzhauser-Peters holds a Bachelor's degree from the University of Cincinnati and Master's degree from Miami University. She has 25 years of experience working in public schools in Special Education and as a Speech-language pathologist, as a Supervisor, and currently as a Curriculum Consultant. Her areas of expertise are language, literacy, and intervention.

The authors met at the Warren County Educational Service Center in Lebanon, Ohio. There they developed and implemented a host of language arts initiatives including a large-scale writing assessment. They have given numerous presentations on the five communication processes and Ohio's proficiencies.

Acknowledgements

Show What You Know® Publishing acknowledges the following for their efforts in making this material available for students, parents, and teachers.

Cindi Englefield, President/Publisher
Eloise Boehm-Sasala, Vice President/Managing Editor
Mercedes Baltzell, Production Editor
Scott D. Stuckey, Editor
Lainie Burke, Desktop Publisher/Assistant Editor
Jennifer Harney, Illustrator/Cover Designer

Content Reviewers:
Kathie Christian, Proofreader
Erica T. Klingerman, Proofreader

Printer:
McNaughton & Gunn, Inc.

Table of Contents

Table of Contents

Table of Contents

Foreword

We are fortunate to have worked with many wonderful educators and students in the years before writing this book. For the past ten years, we have examined over 40,000 student papers that were responses to prompts that provided students with on-demand writing tasks.

In our work, we have observed that many students have the ideas and motivation to complete the writing tasks asked of them but are unable to demonstrate appropriate writing skills. We have learned, through 12 years of large-scale writing assessment, that students often fall short in the organization of their thoughts and ideas. It was apparent in many cases that students did not have specific or organized structures "inside their heads" to plan their writing. As a result, their writing did not address the mode, was disorganized, shifted among purposes, and had weak endings. To improve students' organizational skills, we developed a graphic organizer for each of the 11 modes of writing. We tied each mode to one of five communication processes – narration, description, directions, explanation, and persuasion.

The model lesson format found in this book was demonstrated to classroom teachers with significant numbers of students at risk. These teachers used the model lesson format, modeling technique, and graphic organizers with their "at risk" students. After working for seven to eight months, these teachers found that their students' writing scores were the best in the building! Critical to this success was the ability of the classroom teacher to model the use of the graphic organizers over and over again, using clear examples for each mode of writing as a model.

Included in this book are descriptions of the five communication processes and 11 modes of writing, 22 model lessons, 22 prompts written with a purpose and an audience, 11 graphic organizers, student checklists, additional writing prompts, and a description of where students typically break down in the writing process. In addition, selected modes have picture boards, planning questions, or planning guides to help students plan with pictures or words.

The tools found in this book will serve students well as they work to improve their writing skills.

Introduction

Primary Purpose

The primary purpose of this book is to enable students to understand the unique features of each of the five communication processes (narrative, descriptive, direction, explanation, and persuasive) and to practice 11 modes of writing.

What are Graphic Organizers?

Graphic organizers provide students with an organizational framework to help them plan their thinking and organize their thoughts. The use of graphic organizers increases the reader's and the writer's comprehension of the text by providing a map to:

- find connections,
- organize large amounts of information,
- brainstorm ideas, and
- make decisions.

Each graphic organizer in this program shows the key parts of the communication process and the relationship of these parts to the whole.

The greatest challenge some students face is the ability to organize their writing into an orderly framework that is understood by the reader. In both reading and writing, students are asked to interpret and to comprehend meaning. The graphic organizer is a tool that can assist students during the reading and writing processes. While reading with the graphic organizer, students can increase their comprehension by using the graphic organizer to trace the organization of the reading selection. While writing with the graphic organizer, the students can place their own ideas and thoughts into a structure that fits the purpose of the prompt.

Using Graphic Organizers to Succeed

This book provides first- and second-grade classroom teachers with a lesson-plan framework for teaching writing skills to promote student success.

Five specific communication processes (narration, description, direction, explanation, and persuasion) have been selected and paired with specific graphic organizers for instructional use.

To serve as an instructional aid, an animal has been paired with each of the five communication processes to help students visualize beginning, middle, and end. The five communication processes can be further broken down into 11 writing types (modes). (A description of each mode can be found in Preface One.) In order for students to be successful writers, they must be skillful in responding to 11 different modes of writing.

- narrative is paired with a dog graphic

- explanation is paired with a monkey graphic

- descriptive is paired with a parrot graphic

- persuasive is paired with an owl graphic

- direction is paired with a caterpillar graphic

Successful Results with Graphic Organizers

We have seen significant improvement when graphic organizers were used in both regular classroom instruction and large-scale, on-demand writing assessments. Students are able to understand information, to organize their thoughts, and to stay focused on their writing.

When the appropriate graphic organizer is used, teachers are able to trace a student's thinking during the planning stages of writing. After students use the graphic organizer, we see an improved organizational structure in their work with a clear beginning, middle, and end. Students are able to write to the purpose of the mode even when the students' final products are not fully developed. Using graphic organizers allows teachers to see where students break down in the writing process so that intervention can be planned.

Targeted Areas to Improve

Through our experiences in scoring and reflecting on students' writing samples, we recognize there is a significant need to improve student writing content, organization, and clarity in addressing a prompt. We have observed that student papers often contain problems with:

- shifts among the communication processes (for example, students moved between directions and personal experience narrative),

- ideas presented randomly with neither sequence nor organization, and/or

- no clear ending or sense of closure.

Student Writing Development

We could see the development of wonderful ideas on topics by students when graphic organizers were presented. We found that their holistic scores improved with significant gains in content and organization when:

- the same lesson-plan framework was used for any writing task,

- the graphic organizer was tailored to match the purpose of the writing prompt, and

- the same set of graphic organizers was used over and over again so that students developed consistency when writing to the basic communication processes.

Ways to Use *Write on Target* in Your Writing Program

Write on Target Writing Tools

The *Write on Target* workbook includes seven types of tools for students and teachers to use with 11 modes of writing. The tools consist of models, writing prompts, planning questions, picture boards, planning guides, graphic organizers, and checklists. These tools have been included for teachers to help students accomplish the following:

- develop writing ideas,
- determine purpose and audience,
- organize to plan writing,
- develop writing that includes a beginning, a middle, and an end,
- select vocabulary that matches the communication mode, and
- use the checklist to evaluate the effectiveness of the writing.

Guidelines for Using the Models

The 22 models presented for the 11 writing modes represent examples that demonstrate the language features unique to each mode. These models are to be used for students to read and to analyze. These models are not intended as representative of the work expected of students in the first and second grades. However, with many exposures to good models and consistent use of graphic organizers, students' writing will reflect the development of various features of the mode. It is critical that the developing writer be exposed only to models that are error-free. Models should clearly demonstrate the purpose, the organization, the use of supporting details, and the writing conventions that teachers would like to see in students' writing.

Guidelines for Using the Writing Prompts

The 22 writing prompts given for the writing lessons are designed to be suggested topics for students to demonstrate their ability to write for a specific purpose and audience. The assignments can be used as topics for times when teachers and students write together for guided practice or for independent work. Certain assignments could be selected for assessment, for placement in a student's writing portfolio, or even for publication in the classroom and beyond. The topics can even be adapted to be part of a Writer's Workshop approach to teaching writing.

Guidelines for Using the Planning Questions

Planning questions are part of the fictional narrative, personal narrative, retelling, journal, and informational report modes. These questions guide students and teachers to think about some of the critical features of the mode. Teachers/students can

- answer some or all of the questions.
- write words or draw pictures to answer the questions.
- discuss answers orally.

Guidelines for Using the Picture Boards

Picture boards are provided for the fictional narrative, personal narrative, retelling, and journal modes. At various times, students may want to draw pictures of their ideas. Their pictures may represent characters, events, or even descriptive details of a story or a writing mode. Teachers and students can choose to develop ideas for writing through pictures or words. The choice can be made to use only pictures on the picture board, only words on the graphic organizer, or any combination of the two.

Guidelines for Using the Planning Guide

Planning guides are part of the descriptive letter, persuasive letter, thank-you note, direction (How to Do Something/How to Go Somewhere), invitation, and summary modes.

Students and teachers can choose from vocabulary specific to the mode, such as direction words or types of greetings in letters. With the summary mode, the planning guide provides steps to follow to think through the summary process.

Guidelines for Using the Graphic Organizer

Write on Target has graphic organizers that match 11 modes of writing. Each graphic organizer was developed to incorporate those components of the mode that make it unique and different from the others. The goal in having students use the graphic organizers is to provide them with an organizational framework that allows them to learn and to integrate the characteristics and components of each mode. The goal is to use the same graphic organizer any time the student is asked to write or to speak using that particular mode. If students are asked to use a different graphic organizer each time they write or speak, the purpose is defeated.

Students may not understand how to use graphic organizers initially. They often use the graphic organizers to write out their entire paper rather than as a tool for planning.

- Model the use of the graphic organizer by thinking through the planning of a written piece (think out loud).
- Model the completion of the graphic organizer by inserting a word, a phrase, a picture, or an abbreviation in each box. This modeling process needs to occur over and over again (think out loud).
- Explain to students the purpose of the graphic organizer. Students need to know that their time and energy should be reserved for writing their own pieces.
- Model how to transfer thoughts organized on the graphic organizer into a written piece (think out loud).

Guidelines for Using the Checklists

The checklist at the end of each of the writing prompts provides a list of features that students and teachers can use to review and to evaluate the effectiveness of the writing while editing or revising.

Use the Tools with Scaffolded Instructional Strategies

These tools are designed for use by students at various stages in the writing process and/or during the guided practice phase of a lesson using the scaffolded instructional strategies listed here (see page 14):

- Teacher writes as students talk.
- Teacher and students write together.
- Teacher guides as students write.
- Students write independently.

In addition, Write on Target can be used in the following ways:

1. as a major component of a **yearlong writing program**. Students would complete two prompts for each of the 11 modes in either grade one or grade two.

2. as a **pre- or post-assessment** for each of the 11 modes of writing for a particular grade level.

3. as an **assessment portfolio** that would move with each student from grade one to grade two (11 prompts covering the 11 modes in grade one; 11 prompts covering the 11 modes in grade two).

4. as a **bank of prompts** that supports regular classroom instruction.

5. as support for concentrated **standardized-test preparation** programs.

6. as a **summer school writing program** or as part of an **intervention program**.

7. as **on-demand writing tasks** for individual practice.

Ways to Use *Write on Target* in Your Reading Program

In addition to aiding in the writing process, the graphic organizers can be used to assist with comprehension during the reading process. The graphic organizers will assist students in covering the following skills to improve reading comprehension.

1. Comprehend Fiction and Nonfiction Selections

- to assess what a student knows about a topic (prior knowledge)
- to organize ideas in reading materials
- to gain an understanding of the structure of a specific communication process (purpose)
- to guide and to focus students' thinking during class discussion of student writing or reading materials

2. Interpret Fiction and Nonfiction Selections

- to facilitate text comprehension by making new connections
- to see how things are related
- to organize personal reactions, thoughts, and feelings
- to create original products to fit a specific communication process (purpose)

Modes Of Writing

What Writing Skills Should Students Have?

In first and second grade, students are developing the ability to write for a variety of purposes and to a variety of audiences. These 11 modes of writing prepare students to write for school success, and they prepare students for the skills of life.

We believe that first and second grade students should be introduced to all 11 modes at their developmental level throughout the year. Some of the modes, such as persuasion, are often thought to be too difficult for first and second graders. However, as students develop, their language for each of the writing modes develops simultaneously. If you have dealt with a young child intent on persuading you to do something, you know that children are able to persuade with compelling spoken reasons.

In first- and second-grade classrooms, students might be asked to persuade others to read a book they enjoyed. The persuasion may go something like this.

> I really liked the book because it made me laugh.
> (Name of character) solves problems in funny ways by _____.
> I think you would enjoy the book.

As students are exposed to appropriate models, they will continue to develop their writing skills. Their writing skills will become more complex with clearly defined beginnings, middles, and ends as well as supporting details.

These 11 modes of writing can be used at different points of the year with varying time frames. You might choose to use two or three of the modes as part of a longer writing lesson with fictional narratives, personal experience narratives, and descriptive letters. You may want to do a shared class writing with an invitation or a thank-you note. Journal writing could be part of a daily writing experience. You may use informational reports, directions, retellings, and summaries as part of an integrated approach for writing in social studies, mathematics, health, or science.

A curriculum map of the writing modes is included on page 26. Teachers can use this map to determine when each mode will be taught and/or assessed.

Eleven Modes of Writing

1. **Fictional Narrative** – a piece of writing that has a title, named characters, and events that detail what happens. A fictional narrative establishes an inferred or explicit problem. It has a beginning, a middle, and an end. A fictional narrative is a made-up story that could appear to be true to the reader.

2. **Personal Experience Narrative** – a piece of writing that has a title and a beginning, a middle, and an end. It is a story based on the student's own life experiences, and it discusses who was there, when it happened, and where it happened. A personal experience narrative has to be believable but does not have to be true, just realistic.

3. **Retelling** – a piece of writing that starts with the beginning of the story and retells the story in the same order as the original. A retelling is written with a beginning, a middle, and an end. It includes characters who are in the story and uses details from the story. A retelling is written in the student's own words and does not include additional details that were not part of the original story.

4. **Journal** – a piece of writing that includes a date and a description of the writer's feelings, or the sights, the sounds, the events, or the people the writer has encountered. Most often, the audience is the writer.

5. **Letter** – a piece of writing that has a specific form which includes a greeting, a body, and a closing. A letter addresses a specific audience and establishes a written connection with that audience.

6. **Directions** – a piece of writing that explains how to do something or how to go somewhere. It clearly describes the materials that are needed to complete the task and uses step-by-step order. Directions may be written in paragraph form or line by line. A starting point and an ending point are included.

7. **Invitation** – a piece of writing that can be in letter format. An invitation includes the purpose of the invitation, who is writing the invitation, who is being invited, where and when the event takes place, and any other important information.

8. **Thank-You Note** – a piece of writing that is written in the form of a letter and includes a greeting, a body, and a closing. A thank-you note explains what the writer is thankful for and why.

Eleven Modes of Writing (continued)

9. **Summary** – a piece of writing identifying what a text selection is about. A summary states the main ideas of a text selection. It does not include information that is not important. A summary has fewer details than a retelling.

10. **Informational Report** – a piece of nonfiction writing that is based on researched facts but is written in the student's own words. It is presented in an organized format with a beginning, a middle, and an end. It can cover a wide variety of topics. The purpose of an informational piece of writing is to inform the reader about what the author has learned.

11. **Persuasive Letter** – a piece of writing that is written in the form of a letter and includes a greeting, a body, and a closing. A persuasive letter expresses the writer's opinion and explains why it is important by using facts, examples, or reasons. It also states what the writer would like to see happen.

Write on Target and the Writing Process

All of the tools in *Write on Target* can be used to support the writing process. A writing lesson can start and end in one 10-minute instructional session or can extend over a week depending on your purpose for the writing lesson. The steps of the writing process and the *Write on Target* tools that support those steps are shown on the next page.

Steps in the Writing Process	Write on Target Tools
1. Prewrite Discuss the purpose of the communication process (narration, description, directions, explanation, and persuasion) Discuss the text features of the communication mode (fictional narrative, descriptive letter—select on of the 11 modes) • vocabulary often used • structure (paragraph vs. date, closing) • essential features (narratives: characters, problems, ending) Discuss the audience and the purpose of the communication • vocabulary choices • sentence structure	**1. Prewrite** Models included Suggested texts Suggestions for additional sources of models Student papers
2. Plan Think of ideas to write about Discuss and model ways to get ideas Choose ideas Organize ideas	**2. Plan** Planning questions Planning guides Story board Graphic organizers Writing prompts Ideas for writing prompts
3. Write Write rough drafts on lined paper	**3. Write** Lined paper provided
4. Check and Edit Reread for understanding Use the checklist as a guide to reread	**4. Check and Edit** Checklist for writing
5. Publishing Determine which writing pieces will be published (Note: not all writing pieces should be published)	**5. Publishing** Teacher and students select writings to be published. Publishing formats include: • chart paper in classroom, • work hung outside the room, • student newsletters, • classroom anthologies, and/or • school publishing centers.

Explaining the Model Lesson: The Big Picture

The Model Lesson

There are four major components key to any good lesson that incorporates graphic organizers. These four components are:

1. **Prior Knowledge** – to determine students' prior knowledge about the topic, purpose, or task of the lesson.

2. **Model** – to model the use of the graphic organizer through class discussion with the thinking process modeled aloud as the organizer is completed.

3. **Guided Practice** – to provide guided practice by presenting a task for students to complete that matches the purpose of the graphic organizer you want to teach.

4. **Independent Practice** – to provide independent practice so students can complete on-demand writing tasks that are organized according to the purpose.

Defining Each Component of the Model Lesson

I. Determining Prior Knowledge of Students

Students must make personal connections with the purpose of the material being presented. Establishing a student's familiarity with the material is important for interpreting and comprehending meaning and for ultimately retaining information. The following questions can be used with any lesson to tap into the prior knowledge of the whole class or of an individual student.

1. What do you know about _____? (The student response provides the teacher with an assessment of what the student knows prior to the lesson.)

2. Where do you see _____ in your life? (The student response helps to establish the importance of the task for now and for the future.)

Both of these questions show how students are connected with the material. This process is important for the retention of information. Students need to make connections themselves.

Sample Questions to Tap Prior Knowledge:

- Does anyone know what a narrative is?
- What do we know about narratives?
- What are some parts of a narrative?
- What is the narrative's purpose? or audience?
- Who reads or writes narratives?
- Where do you see narratives every day?
- What does personal mean?
- What is a personal narrative?

II. Modeling

Modeling or demonstrating the thinking process for the use of the selected graphic organizer is an important component of any lesson. Modeling must be done frequently because it is the part of the lesson by which students construct meaning.

There are different types of modeling.

1. Demonstrating the thinking process used in completing a graphic organizer
   - Teacher writes as students talk.
   - Teacher and students write together.
   - Teacher guides students as they write.

2. Providing student writing samples keyed to the developmental writing rubric (The writing rubric can be found on page 20.)

All types of modeling must be done frequently. Time is well spent during the modeling phase of the lesson. Modeling clarifies the task and enables the student to internalize the standard.

The model needs to match the purpose of the writing task the students will complete. Written models can be obtained from a variety of sources (see chart on page 18). Once you become aware of the writing modes, you and your students will be able to select written models from a variety of sources.

- newspapers
- trade books
- textbooks
- student generated models*

* Over time, develop a bank of students' responses that are good examples of the different types of writing modes; include different levels of the developmental writing rubric.

III. Guided Practice

During guided practice, the teacher should provide various levels of support for students as needed.

Scaffolded Instruction

Teacher writes as students talk.	Teacher and students write together.
Teacher uses the graphic organizer to record and to guide students' spoken ideas. • Teacher calls attention to the characteristics of the communication process and to the features of the writing mode. • The richness of a student's oral language can be captured for instructional use. • The process can be used to highlight onsets, rimes, sounds, letters, and word-making. • Teacher increases student awareness of spacing, directionality, capitalization, and punctuation.	Teacher and students take turns writing. Students write what they can with teacher guidance and completion. • Students actually take part in the writing at the developmental level. • Instruction can be organized for the class as a whole, for a small group, or for an individual. • Teacher demonstrates the characteristics of the communication process and features of the writing mode.
Teacher guides students as they write.	**Students write independently.**
Teacher models how to use the graphic organizer. Teacher discusses or highlights characteristics of the communication process (*e.g.,* narrative, descriptive, explanation) and the features of the writing mode (*e.g.,* fictional narrative, informational report). Students then plan and write their own pieces with teacher guidance and support. • Students are directly taught the mode and the use of the graphic organizer for planning and organizing written pieces. • Teacher assists students with idea production and organization as students compose their individual pieces. • Teacher addresses the developmental needs of each student.	Students write independently when provided with a writing prompt that must be completed during a specified amount of time with no teacher support. This type of writing is often part of large-scale writing assessments. Papers are usually considered rough drafts. Opportunities can be provided for selected pieces to be edited, revised, and published. • Each student's writing ability (including creativity) can be evaluated for strengths and weaknesses. • Teacher can review student papers to determine instructional focus. • A pool of papers provides a rich source of models for revision.

IV. Independent Practice for Benchmark Assessment

Provide an authentic task for students to complete that matches what it is you want to teach. For example, have students write a persuasive letter to the principal regarding an issue facing the school, or ask students to write a set of directions to be followed.

After considerable guided practice, provide students with many opportunities to engage in independent practice with on-demand writing prompts. Sample prompts are included at the end of each chapter of this book.

Independent practice is an on-demand task that provides students with a test-like writing experience. During independent practice, students should be given a graphic organizer, a writing prompt with a specific purpose, a writing model (optional), lined paper, and a writing checklist. It is important that teachers provide enough time for students to complete the writing task.

If independent practice is going to be used for assessment purposes, no teacher or peer assistance should be provided to students. No reference materials can be used. On-demand writing assessment is different from lessons that take students through all stages of the writing process. Student papers generated through lessons are considered rough drafts and placed on the developmental writing rubric. It is critical that students be provided with this type of task on many occasions throughout the school year.

The on-demand writing task is designed so that students can choose to use either print or cursive handwriting. The students should choose the format that is most comfortable to them. Every attempt should be made to determine the meaning and the content of each student's paper. Legibility issues should be minimized whenever possible.

After the students have completed this type of independent practice for assessment, it is the role of the teacher to return to the model lesson and to cycle through the lesson again before the next assessment is presented to the class.

The curriculum map of the writing modes included on page 26 can be used to map out the writing modes that will be assessed and when each one will be assessed.

The Model Lesson at a Glance:
Putting It All Together, Step by Step

Writing activities for each writing mode are arranged step by step in the Teacher Edition and in the Student Workbook. The following steps are derived from the four components of the Model Lesson. Each time you teach a lesson, you may want to refer to these steps. This model lesson guide is directly matched to the writing activities in the chapters that follow.

Prior Knowledge

Before you begin, ask students, "What do you know about _____ (*insert one of the writing modes, e.g., fictional narrative*)? Where have you seen this in your life?"

Model

Step 1:
- Introduce a model text selection that is typical of the writing mode you are describing.
- Read the model and highlight its features.
- Show the graphic organizer that corresponds to the writing mode. (Full-sized graphic organizers can be found throughout the Student Workbook.)
- Use the model text selection to complete the graphic organizer.
- Explain how the graphic organizer should be used by completing the graphic organizer on an overhead or by providing each student with a personal copy.
- As a class, demonstrate the completion of the graphic organizer using a think-out-loud technique.

Step 2: Discuss the characteristics of the communication process you are introducing.

The Model Lesson at a Glance: Putting It All Together, Step by Step

Guided Practice

Step 3: Introduce the prompt students will be addressing as well as the appropriate graphic organizer. Students should think about how they will address the prompt.

Step 4: Students will complete the graphic organizer based on the prompt. The graphic organizer will help students arrange their thoughts.

Step 5: Each student will complete the writing activity based on the prompt and the information he or she has organized with the graphic organizer.

Step 6: The checklist provided in this section shows what a student's best paper must have. Students should use this checklist as a guideline for their responses.

Independent Practice

Step 7: Once students have completed the first six steps, they are ready for independent practice. Provide students with on-demand writing tasks. Refer to the additional prompts, specific to each writing mode, found at the end of each chapter of this book. (For more information on independent practice, refer to pages 14 and 15.)

Step 8: The final step is to evaluate the student papers based on the developmental writing rubric. Students should become familiar with the features of the *Write on Target* Developmental Writing Rubric. (See page 20.)

The Five Communication Processes
Matched with Eleven Writing Modes

Communication Process	Eleven Writing Modes	Sources of Models
Narrative	Fictional Narratives	magazines, big books, literature-based reading series, puppet shows, narrative poetry
	Personal Experience Narratives	newspapers, diaries, journals
	Retellings	personal conversations, book reports, news updates
Descriptive*	Journals	diaries, journals, science reports, advertisements
	Letters	letters from family, pen pals, authors, politicians, peers, classroom magazines
Direction	Directions	recipes, stage directions, maps, travel brochures, games
	Invitations	weddings, birthdays, parties, informal formats
Explanation	Informational Reports	show and tell, science and social studies textbooks, newspapers, classroom encyclopedias and classroom magazines
	Summaries	movie reviews, book jackets, learning journals
	Thank-You Notes	thank-you notes from teachers, principals, parents
Persuasive	Persuasive Letters	newspapers, magazines, advertisements, commercials

* Note: The ability to describe is an important skill embedded in many of the communication processes and writing modes.

Evaluating and Assessing Student Work

The *Write on Target* Developmental Writing Rubric on page 20 is a scoring rubric that describes the four types of writing you might see among your students' work. This rubric establishes criteria that can be used to determine developmental levels of student papers by describing the qualities the papers exhibit.

Using the Write on Target Developmental Writing Rubric

As you examine your students' papers, ask these questions to help you and your students diagnose the strengths and challenges of their writing.

1. Where does this paper fit on a scale of 4 to 1? Using the descriptions on each level of the rubric, place each student paper in a level 4, 3, 2, or 1 category (fluent to early writer). The number of papers in each category will vary from assignment to assignment. The ultimate goal is for all students' papers to match the descriptive features of a level 4 paper as students develop their writing skills and strategies. Keep in mind students' writing development will vary.

2. As you examine each paper individually, ask
   - what is this student able to do?
   - what are the student's writing strengths?
   - what is one writing focus that would help the student's writing be even more communicative?

This holistic scoring process does not have to be completed on every paper produced by your students. You will want to focus on selected assignments to analyze and to diagnose your students' writings.

Write on Target Developmental Writing Rubric

Level 4 – Fluent Writer

- Demonstrates a clear sense of audience and purpose
- Has a clear beginning, middle, and end
- Flows with consistent organization
- Includes supportive details, descriptive language, and interesting vocabulary
- Has various sentence patterns and lengths

Level 3 – Beginning Writer

- Considers audience and purpose
- Shows organization of a beginning, a middle, and an end
- Uses basic sentence patterns and structures
- Attempts to use descriptive words and supporting details
- Includes correct punctuation, capitalization, and spelling patterns in most attempts

Level 2 – Emerging Writer

- Demonstrates a beginning sense of purpose and audience
- Shows beginning awareness of the communication mode
- Has sentences that are short and simple; some may be fragmented
- Uses invented spelling that is logical
- Attempts use of capitalization and punctuation

Level 1 – Early Writer

- Lacks a clear purpose in the writing (the message may be dictated by the student and scribed by the teacher)
- May use single letters, one word, or an occasional short sentence or phrase
- Shows some evidence of sound/symbol relationship between the writings and student drawings
- Uses letter strings to represent words or entire ideas
- May use high frequency words (the, an, me) or words copied from word walls or classroom environment
- May include attempts at invented spellings

Developmental Writing Stages

The following describes the stages that children go through as they develop their writing abilities. As teachers evaluate children's writing, they may note key indicators of a particular stage of development. As children's writing develops, you may note the use of characteristics from more than one stage of writing. It is difficult to assign a specific grade level to developing writers. In the early grades, you may observe children writing at all four stages.

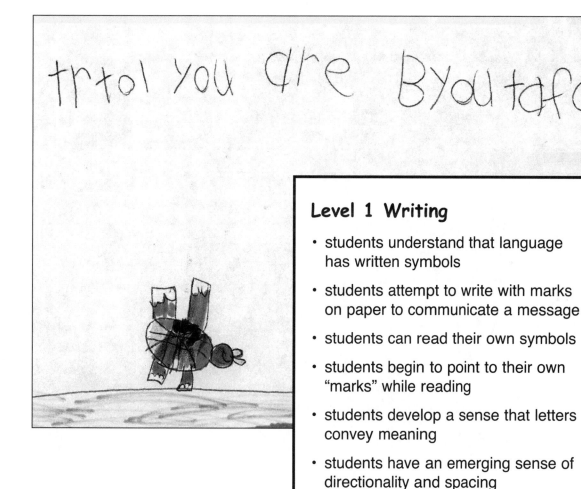

Level 1 Writing

- students understand that language has written symbols

- students attempt to write with marks on paper to communicate a message

- students can read their own symbols

- students begin to point to their own "marks" while reading

- students develop a sense that letters convey meaning

- students have an emerging sense of directionality and spacing

- students may use real letters or approximations

Level 2 Writing

- students realize that speech can be written

- students realize that English is written from left to right

- students' writings contain a greater number of recognizable letters and words

- students use the most obvious sounds of words and rely on phonetic representations

- students understand that each written word corresponds to a spoken word

- students write lists, letters, and individual messages

- students can "read back" their own writing

- students use left-to-right and top-to-bottom spacing

What ants do
ants make tonols in the san
and store there food.
there are eite stil alive
there are more tule then
there were, there ore stil ants,

Once there was a little puppy. Puppy lived with a farmer on a farm. Puppy **One** day got board and wondered off into the woods. All the animals were woried, "What if he's lost," said the cow. "What if he's in danger," said another. But Puppy was having the best time of his life.

Level 3 Writing

- students begin to consider audience and purpose

- students have an emerging sentence sense

- students can use writing conventions, spell commonly used words, and use beginning and ending punctuation

- students can write to a variety of communication modes

- students use basic sentence structures

- students can explain the purpose of communication

- students are able to experiment with writing based on the written and the spoken models around them

Level 4 Writing

- students have a sense of audience and purpose that is evident
- students' writings have a clear beginning, middle, and end
- students' writings have an organization and flow
- students' writings include supporting details, descriptive language, and interesting vocabulary
- students' writing includes varied sentence patterns and sentence length

Fuerte

On a small boat there was a man that had a cat named Ginger. They both lived together on a boat called Blue Horn. They both found Blue Horn to be a fine sturdy boat. One night right before bedtime. (All of the sudden!) Roar! There was a scream, Ahh! The cat hissed with all his might. The man ran to get a light on! But he tripped over something, and he heard a snap! He jumped to his feet and ran Then he reached a lamp. He tried to turn it on. He found that he tripped over the power cord. So he found a lantern and reached out and shined it on where the sounds were coming from. What he saw filled him with fright! For there was a monster. They called it Fuerte. It had five powerful arms. It was bigger than a blue whale! It was so slimy it looked like it could slide across a sandy beach without a grain of sand stuck to it.

* Note: This is a portion of the student's completed composition.

Design Your Own Writing Prompts

Guidelines to Consider

1. **A clear purpose must be specified.** Choose the writing mode you want to test and tell students what they are expected to do. Use words such as "describe," "persuade," or "retell" in the directions. Keep the prompt as simple as possible. Prompts should be composed of words your students can easily read and understand. The writing test should not become a reading test.

2. **The audience should be indicated.** The audience should be a person or a group students would feel comfortable addressing. Often, for the purposes of the writing assessment, teacher scorers are the audience.

3. **Students should have a solid prior knowledge base about the topic before they begin writing.** The subject matter of the writing prompt should be within the realm of each student's experience and should not involve emotionally charged issues that would distract from the writing task. For example, not all students have visited Canada. Asking students to describe the landscape of Canada would be unfair to those students who have not experienced the Canadian landscape firsthand. An alternative might be to ask students to describe their idea of a beautiful landscape.

4. **The evaluation criteria and prompt checklist should be reviewed with students before administering the on-demand writing task.** The scoring rubric should not be a mystery to the students. Students need to develop a clear understanding of the standards and scoring procedures. We have found that students become excellent scorers when trained to use the rubric.

Curriculum Map of the Writing Modes

MODES	AUG.	SEPT.	OCT.	NOV.	DEC.	JAN.	FEB.	MAR.	APR.	MAY	JUNE
Fictional Narrative											
Personal Experience Narrative											
Retelling											
Informational											
Journal											
Summary											
Directions											
Invitation											
Descriptive Letter											
Persuasive Letter											
Thank-You Note											

The Narrative Communication Process
(Fictional Narrative, Personal Experience Narrative, and Retelling)

The purposes of this chapter include:

1 Showing how the narrative communication process links to the writing modes.

2 Discussing the purpose and features of a fictional narrative, a personal experience narrative, and a retelling.

3 Offering teaching tips on where students break down in the narrative communication process.

4 Providing ideas for the development of additional writing prompts for the fictional narrative, personal experience narrative, and retelling.

The following teaching tools are provided for a **fictional narrative**, a **personal experience narrative**, and a **retelling**: planning questions, picture boards, graphic organizers, two writing prompts, and student checklists.

What is the Narrative Communication Process?

The purpose of a narrative is to tell a story. A fictional narrative is a made-up story. A personal experience narrative is an account of an event that could have happened to the writer in real life. A retelling recounts a story with the same sequence of events and details that appear in the original version.

Features of a Fictional Narrative
- Is a made-up story that has a central problem

Features of a Personal Experience Narrative
- Is typically told in the first person ("I")
- Focuses on an event that could have happened to the writer in real life

Features of a Retelling
- Restates the story
- Does not add details based on the writer's personal perceptions or opinions
- Is told in the writer's own words; it is not copied

Narrative Communication information for students can be found on page 1 of the *Write on Target* Student Workbook.

Correlation of Narrative Communication to the Writing Modes

Fictional narrative – a piece of writing that has a title, named characters, and events that detail what happens. A fictional narrative establishes an inferred or explicit problem. It has a beginning, a middle, and an end. A fictional narrative is a made-up story that could appear to be true to the reader.

Personal experience narrative – a piece of writing that has a title and a beginning, a middle, and an end. It is a story based on the student's own life experiences, and it discusses who was there, when it happened, and where it happened. A personal experience narrative has to be believable but does not have to be true, just realistic.

Retelling – a piece of writing that starts with the beginning of the story and retells the story in the same order as the original. A retelling is written with a beginning, a middle, and an end. It includes characters that are in the story and uses details from the story. A retelling is written in the student's own words and does not include additional details that were not part of the original story.

Teaching Tips: Where Students Break Down in the Narrative Communication Process

- Students write the story as they would tell it verbally, so it is not organized in a sequential fashion.

- Students make assumptions that the reader has had the same experience. Students leave out information that is essential for the reader.

- Students include too much information that takes away from the storyline.

- Students do not stay with the purpose.

- Students confuse personal experience narrative with fictional narrative. A personal experience narrative should include an experience that could or did happen to the narrator.

- Students write a summary of the story rather than a retelling.

- Students' retellings do not have beginnings, middles, or ends. Students often begin the retelling in the middle of the story and/or leave out major parts of the story.

- Students add details to a retelling that are based on their own perceptions or opinions.

Writing Activity 1: Fictional Narrative (A Made-Up Story)

Step 1 Follow along as the fictional narrative (a made-up story) "Wuffy" is read aloud.

Wuffy

Wuffy was a cute little puppy. He had brown fur and brown eyes. He loved to bark at other dogs, play with his toys, chase his tail, and do all kids of cute "doggy" things. Some people might have thought Wuffy was a very happy puppy. But Wuffy was sad.

Wuffy's home was behind bars in a loud, stinky place called the pound. He wanted to be adopted, and he would have done whatever it took to find a home.

Human after human walked by his cage. Wuffy cried and howled in his loudest bark. "Pick me!" he cried, but no one picked Wuffy.

Wuffy was so tired and sad that he fell asleep on his torn blanket.

While he was sleeping, a young boy visited the pound. He was looking for the perfect puppy. He looked in Wuffy's cage and saw the sleeping dog.

"I'll take this one," the boy said. Wuffy was adopted.

by Alexandra Grizinski

2

Chapter 1

Narrative
(Fictional Narrative, Personal Experience Narrative, and Retelling)

What is a Narrative?

The purpose of a narrative is to tell a story.

A **fictional narrative** is a made-up story. Fictional narratives are not true.

In a **personal experience narrative**, you write about something that has happened to you, or something that could have happened to you in real life.

A **retelling** tells the story again in your own words.

1

FICTIONAL NARRATIVE

Planning Questions for a Made-Up Story

Use pictures or words.

Who are the characters?

Where does the story take place?

When does the story happen?

What happens in the story?

How does the story end?

4

Step 2

Remember, a good fictional narrative (a made-up story) has the following parts.

- a title
- a character or characters you can picture in your mind
- a problem
- a beginning, a middle, and an end

Step 3

Use the following idea to plan your fictional narrative (a made-up story).

> **Tell your teacher a story about your favorite animal. It can be your stuffed animal toy, an animal you have seen, or even a pet.**

Step 4

Answer the planning questions to get ideas for your made-up story. Use your picture board or graphic organizer to help you think through your fictional narrative (a made-up story). You can use pictures or words to plan your fictional narrative (a made-up story).

3

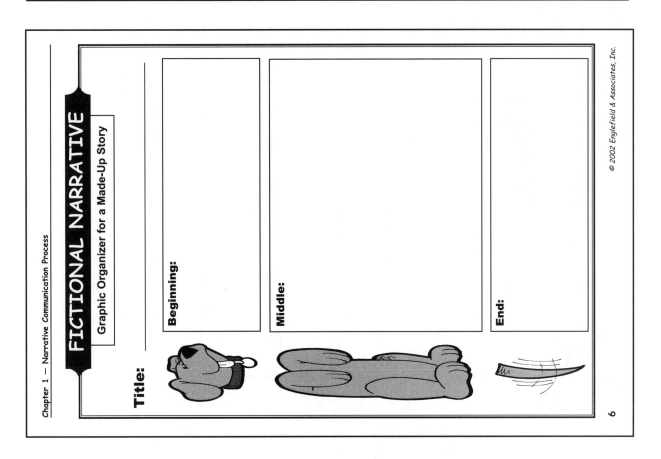

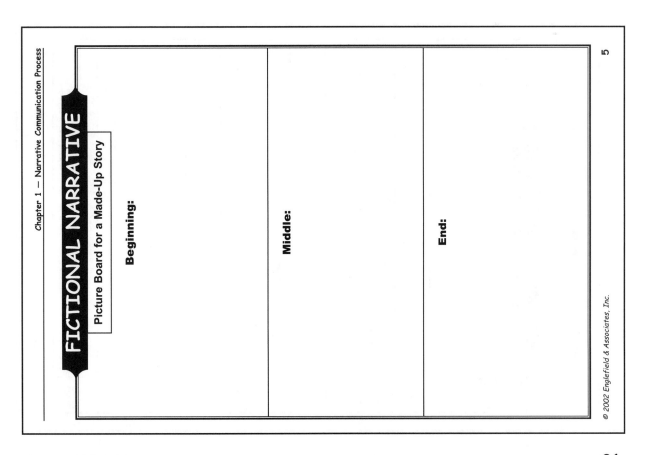

Step **6**

The checklist shows what your best paper must have. Use the checklist below to review your work.

Checklist for Writing Activity 1

- ☐ My story has a title.

- ☐ My story is a made-up story.

- ☐ My characters have names.

- ☐ My story has a beginning, a middle, and an end.

- ☐ I try to spell words correctly.

- ☐ My sentences end with a period, an exclamation point, or a question mark.

- ☐ My sentences begin with capital letters.

8

Write your fictional narrative (a made-up story).

Step **5**

Writing Activity 1

If you need more room, ask a parent or a teacher for another piece of paper.

7

32

Step 2 Remember, a good fictional narrative (a made-up story) has the following parts.

- a title
- a character or characters you can picture in your mind
- a problem
- a beginning, a middle, and an end

Step 3 Use the following idea to plan your fictional narrative (a made-up story).

> **Write a story about a little boy or a little girl who found something. Write the story from your imagination.**

Step 4 Answer the planning questions to get ideas for your made-up story. Use your picture board or graphic organizer to help you think through your fictional narrative (a made-up story). You can use pictures or words to plan your fictional narrative (a made-up story).

10

Writing Activity 2: Fictional Narrative (A Made-Up Story)

Step 1 Follow along as the fictional narrative (a made-up story) "The Treasure Box" is read aloud.

The Treasure Box

Grandmother was a kind woman. She liked to buy presents for Sarah. Sarah was her only granddaughter. Grandmother always brought a white shopping bag to Sarah's house. The white bag held a gift for Sarah. The gift was always perfect.

When Grandmother arrived, she hugged Sarah. She hugged Sarah so tight Sarah could hardly breathe. Sarah looked at the bag. Grandmother smiled and said, "This is for you, my little girl." Grandmother reached into the bag. She pulled out a brown square box.

Sarah took the brown box from her grandmother's hand. The box was covered with small blue and red flowers. Sarah opened it slowly. It was empty.

"This is your treasure box, my little girl. Put your favorite things in the box to keep forever."

The next time Grandmother visited, Sarah was excited to show her the box. Inside the box was a hat covered in small flowers.

"Do you remember this hat?" asked Sarah. "You gave it to me last year. I put my special hat in my special box."

Sarah's grandmother smiled and gave her special granddaughter a big hug.

9

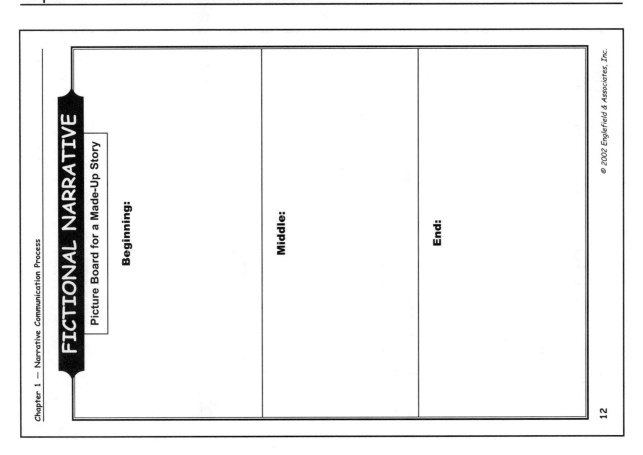

FICTIONAL NARRATIVE

Picture Board for a Made-Up Story

Beginning:

Middle:

End:

12

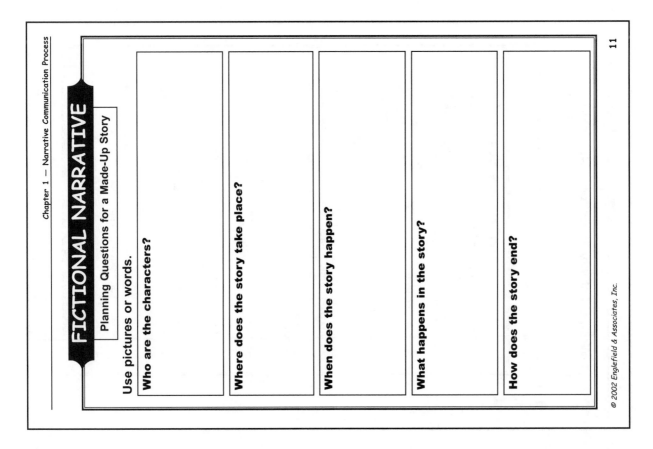

FICTIONAL NARRATIVE

Planning Questions for a Made-Up Story

Use pictures or words.

Who are the characters?

Where does the story take place?

When does the story happen?

What happens in the story?

How does the story end?

11

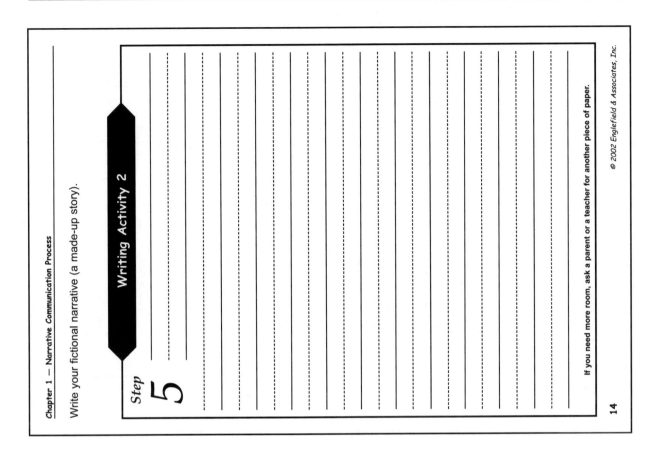

Write your fictional narrative (a made-up story).

Writing Activity 2

Step 5

If you need more room, ask a parent or a teacher for another piece of paper.

14

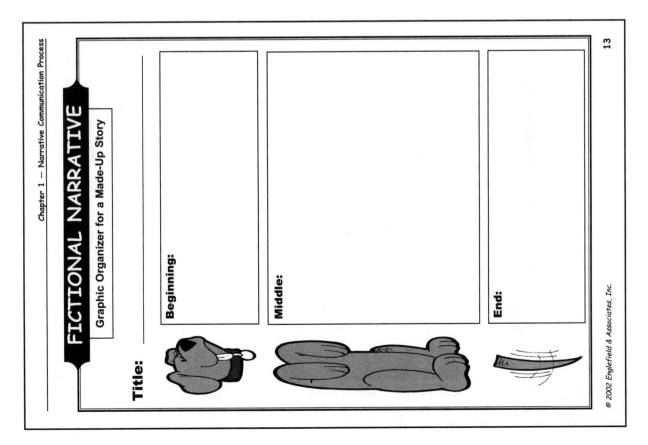

13

FICTIONAL NARRATIVE

Graphic Organizer for a Made-Up Story

Title:

Beginning:

Middle:

End:

Writing Activity 3: Personal Experience Narrative (A Story About Me)

Step 1 Follow along as the personal experience narrative (a story about me) "Leaves" is read aloud.

Leaves

My father decided it was time to rake the fall leaves. We walked into the yard. He handed me a rake that was just my size. I raked and raked the leaves. Slowly, a pile formed. The pile looked soft and inviting. I stepped away from the leaves and dropped the rake.

"Here I come, ready or not!" I took a running start and jumped into the pile of golden leaves. The leaves crunched as I jumped on them. My father laughed as the leaves scattered across the yard.

Dad helped me rake the leaves again. On my last jump, I heard a sound coming from behind the maple tree. "Meow!" A small kitten crawled toward the leaf pile. The kitten and the leaves were the same golden color. When the kitten came closer to the pile, I petted its soft fur.

"Dad! Dad! Look what I found!"

"Well, it looks like we have a new kitten," said Dad.

I took my new friend into the house. I put an old towel in a box to make a bed for the kitten. Mostly, she liked to stay in my lap. She purred and purred.

Later that night, my family thought of a perfect name for my new furry friend. We called our new pet "Leaves."

16

Step 6 The checklist shows what your best paper must have. Use the checklist below to review your work.

Checklist for Writing Activity 2

☐ My story has a title.

☐ My story is a made-up story.

☐ My characters have names.

☐ My story has a beginning, a middle, and an end.

☐ I try to spell words correctly.

☐ My sentences end with a period, an exclamation point, or a question mark.

☐ My sentences begin with capital letters.

15

PERSONAL EXPERIENCE NARRATIVE

Planning Questions for a Story About Me

Use pictures or words.

Who was there?

What happened?

Where did it happen?

When did it happen?

What happened at the end?

18

Step
2

Remember, a good personal experience narrative (a story about me) has the following parts.

- a title
- people you know
- a beginning, a middle, and an end

Step
3

Use the following idea to plan your personal experience narrative (a story about me).

> **Write about something that happened to you that was very funny. It could be something that happened at home, at school, or anywhere else.**

Step
4

Answer the planning questions to get ideas for your story about you. Use your picture board or graphic organizer to help you think through your personal experience narrative (a story about me). You can use pictures or words to plan your personal experience narrative (a story about me).

17

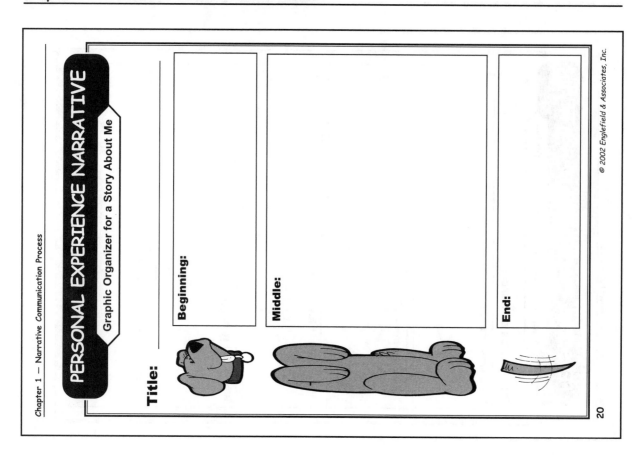

PERSONAL EXPERIENCE NARRATIVE

Graphic Organizer for a Story About Me

Title:

Beginning:

Middle:

End:

20

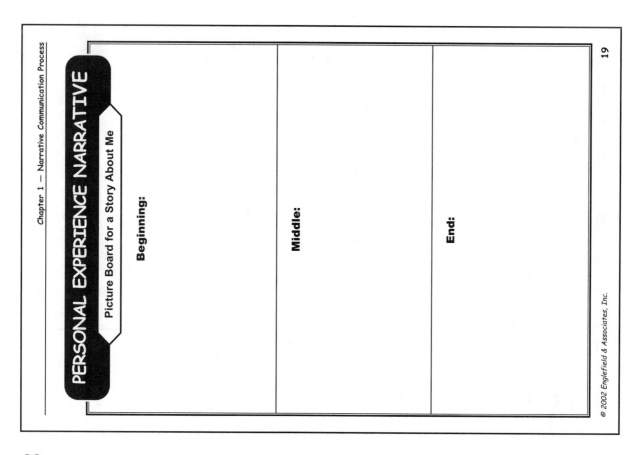

PERSONAL EXPERIENCE NARRATIVE

Picture Board for a Story About Me

Beginning:

Middle:

End:

19

Page 22 (upper)

Step 6

The checklist shows what your best paper must have. Use the checklist below to review your work.

Checklist for Writing Activity 3

☐ My story has a title.

☐ My story is about me.

☐ My story has a beginning, a middle, and an end.

☐ I try to spell words correctly.

☐ I use interesting words.

☐ My sentences end with a period, an exclamation point, or a question mark.

☐ My sentences begin with a capital letter.

☐ Proper names begin with capital letters.

© 2002 Englefield & Associates, Inc.

22

Page 21 (lower)

Write your personal experience narrative (a story about me).

Writing Activity 3

Step 5

_____

_____

_____

_____

_____

_____

_____

_____

_____

_____

_____

_____

If you need more room, ask a parent or a teacher for another piece of paper.

© 2002 Englefield & Associates, Inc.

21

Step 2

Remember, a good personal experience narrative (a story about me) has the following parts.

- a title
- people you know
- a beginning, a middle, and an end

Step 3

Use the following idea to plan your personal experience narrative (a story about me).

> **Write about something that has happened to you. Write your personal experience narrative or story about me as if you were telling the story to a friend or a family member.**

Step 4

Answer the planning questions to get ideas for your story about you. Use your picture board or graphic organizer to help you think through your personal experience narrative (a story about me). You can use pictures or words to plan your personal experience narrative (a story about me).

24

Writing Activity 4: Personal Experience Narrative (A Story About Me)

Step 1

Follow along as the personal experience narrative (a story about me) "The Spooky House" is read aloud.

The Spooky House

When I was five years old, I went to the State Fair. A very scary thing happened to me that day.

After hours of fun with my best friend, something caught my eye. The door to the "Spooky House" stood in front of me. My best friend stood by my side. I felt very brave. If we could go through the "Spooky House" together, I knew I would not be scared. Just as we reached the door, my friend ran to her parents. There I was, entering the dark "Spooky House" without my friend.

When I stepped through the door, I could not see anything. The room was very dark. There was no light. Creepy music was playing. After I took a few steps, a light flashed. I saw a mummy and a ghost. The scene scared me, so I started walking a little faster. I wanted to get away from those two.

As I made my way through the "Spooky House," all I could think about was seeing daylight. Each time a light flashed, I closed my eyes. I didn't want to see any more mummies or ghosts.

Finally, I came to the back door of the "Spooky House." When the sunlight hit my eyes, I saw my friend and her parents. Even though I had been scared, it felt good to go through the house by myself.

by Alexandra Grizinski

23

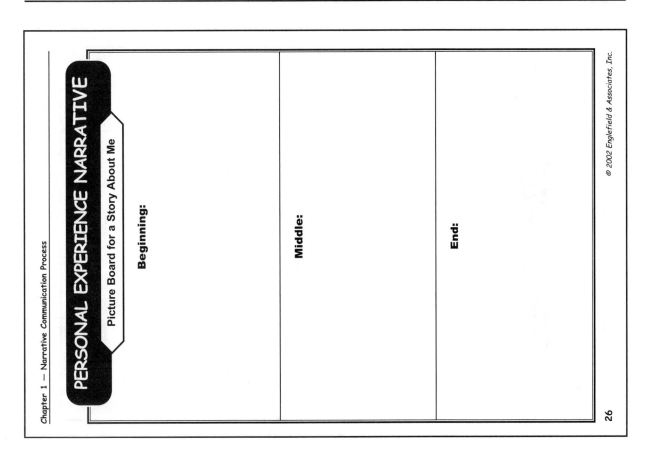

Chapter 1 — Narrative Communication Process

PERSONAL EXPERIENCE NARRATIVE

Picture Board for a Story About Me

Beginning:

Middle:

End:

26

© 2002 Englefield & Associates, Inc.

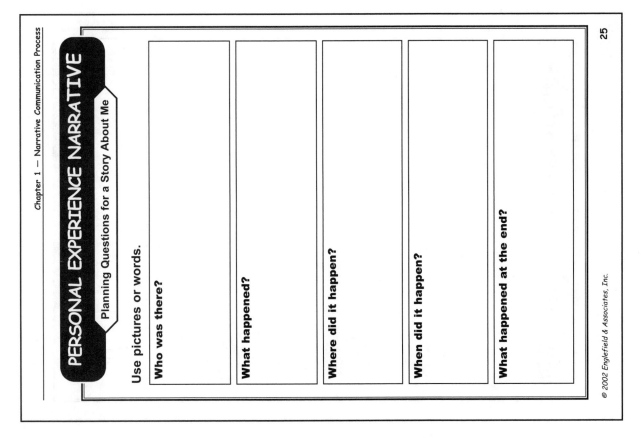

Chapter 1 — Narrative Communication Process

PERSONAL EXPERIENCE NARRATIVE

Planning Questions for a Story About Me

Use pictures or words.

Who was there?

What happened?

Where did it happen?

When did it happen?

What happened at the end?

25

© 2002 Englefield & Associates, Inc.

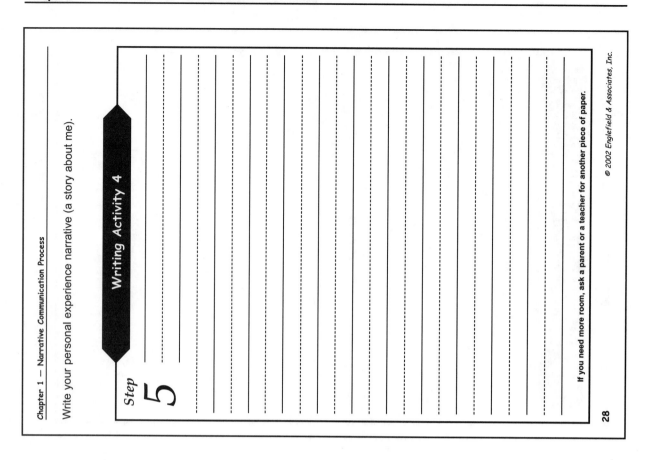

Write your personal experience narrative (a story about me).

Writing Activity 4

Step **5**

If you need more room, ask a parent or a teacher for another piece of paper.

28

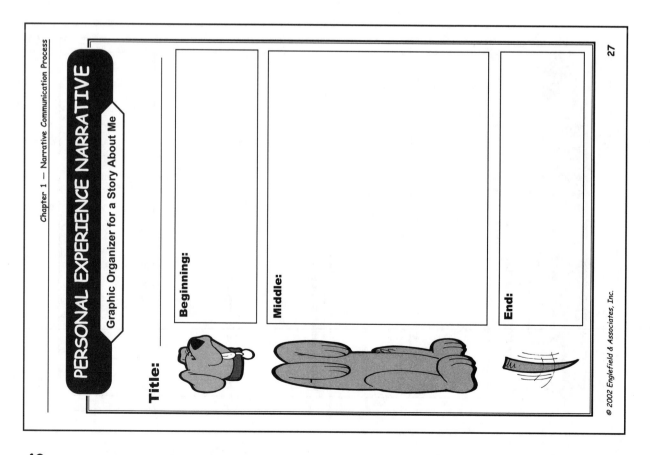

27

PERSONAL EXPERIENCE NARRATIVE

Graphic Organizer for a Story About Me

Title:

Beginning:

Middle:

End:

Writing Activity 5: Retelling
(A Story I Retell in My Own Words)

Step **1**

Follow along as two passages are read. The first passage is a story titled "Butterfly Tummy." The second passage is a retelling (a story I retell in my own words) of "Butterfly Tummy."

Butterfly Tummy

It was an early morning for Andy. He put on his slippers and walked quickly to the kitchen. Today was the big day. Today was Andy's first day at his new school. Andy's mother gave him a bowl of warm oatmeal. There was a little bit of brown sugar on top. Andy stirred his oatmeal. He could only eat half.

Andy felt a little tickle in his stomach. "You're nervous about school," his mom told him. "You have butterflies in your stomach." As he got dressed, he thought about his butterflies. A few minutes later, Andy heard the rumble of the yellow school bus. He grabbed his Mighty Hedgehog lunchbox and ran out the door. He still felt the tickle.

The bus pulled up to the big brick school. Mrs. Hartland greeted Andy as he stepped off the bus. She took his hand and led him to Room 108. The room was full of wonderful sights. Posters hung on the walls. A large carpet filled one corner, and there were books all around. Andy hoped one of the books was about Mighty Hedgehog, his favorite superhero.

"We keep something special over here," said Mrs. Hartland. A glass cage with a net over it sat by the window. Inside the glass cage, five orange and black Monarch butterflies fluttered about. Andy smiled.

"The classroom has butterflies, too," he thought to himself.

30

Step **6**

The checklist shows what your best paper must have. Use the checklist below to review your work.

Checklist for Writing Activity 4

- ☐ My story has a title.

- ☐ My story is about me.

- ☐ My story has a beginning, a middle, and an end.

- ☐ I try to spell words correctly.

- ☐ I use interesting words.

- ☐ My sentences end with a period, an exclamation point, or a question mark.

- ☐ My sentences begin with a capital letter.

- ☐ Proper names begin with capital letters.

29

Step 3 *continued*

Soupy Sings at Sea

Soupy the Singing Seal liked to play in the ocean and spend time with her friends. Every afternoon, Soupy would sing for anyone who would listen. Soupy did not have a pretty voice, but she loved to sing.

One morning, Soupy dove into the water. She was looking for some food. Her brown body moved easily through the salt water. She swam to the ocean floor. She spotted a group of lobsters. Soupy loved to tease the lobsters. They had funny-looking claws and flat tails. Soupy kicked up sand. It swirled in the water. This made it hard for the lobsters to see. Soupy laughed and laughed.

"Why are you always picking on us?" asked Larry the Lobster. Soupy did not have an answer. "If you promise to stop picking on us, I will give you something special," Larry said.

"What can an ugly lobster give to a pretty seal?" Soupy wanted to know.

"You may be pretty, but your voice is not. I can teach you how to sing."

Soupy realized it did not feel good to be picked on. "I promise I will not pick on lobsters ever again," she said. "When can we start my singing lessons?"

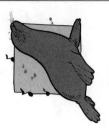

Step 4

Answer the planning questions for the story you retell in your own words. Use your picture board or graphic organizer to help you think through your retelling (a story I retell in my own words). You can use pictures or words to plan your retelling (a story I retell in my own words).

Step 1 *continued*

Retelling of "Butterfly Tummy"

Andy woke up early in the morning. It was his first day of school. He ate half a bowl of oatmeal for breakfast. He felt a tickle in his stomach. His mom told him he had butterflies. He rode the bus to school. He took his lunchbox with him. Mrs. Hartland met Andy when he got off the bus. She took him to his classroom. There was a cage in the classroom. It had butterflies in it. Andy smiled because he and the classroom both had butterflies.

Step 2

Remember, a good retelling (a story I retell in my own words) has the following parts.

- the title of the story
- my own words
- details from the story

Step 3

Use the following idea to plan your retelling (a story I retell in my own words).

Read the story titled "Soupy Sings at Sea" on page 32. Retell the story so the reader will know all the important facts of the story.

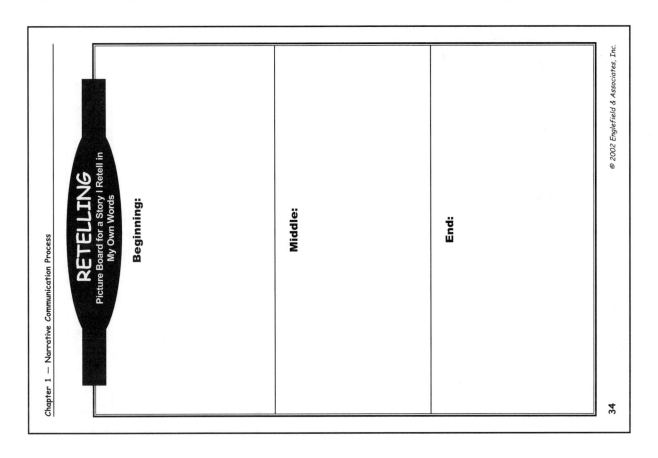

RETELLING
Picture Board for a Story I Retell in
My Own Words

Beginning:

Middle:

End:

34

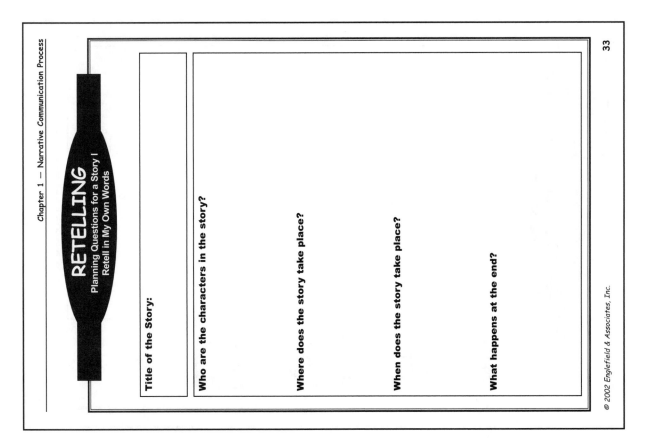

33

RETELLING
Planning Questions for a Story I
Retell in My Own Words

Title of the Story:

Who are the characters in the story?

Where does the story take place?

When does the story take place?

What happens at the end?

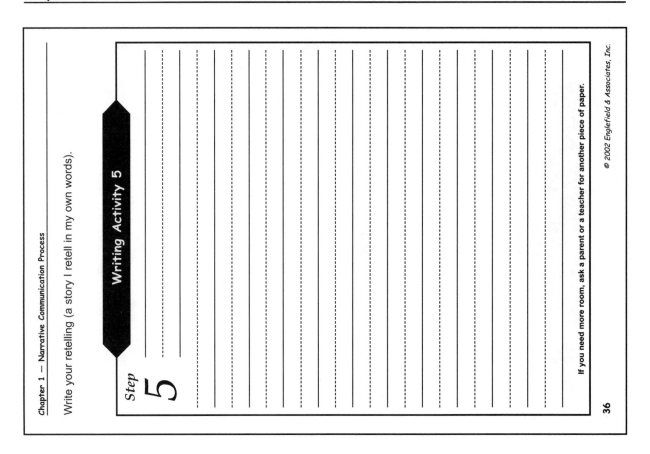

Write your retelling (a story I retell in my own words).

Writing Activity 5

Step **5**

36

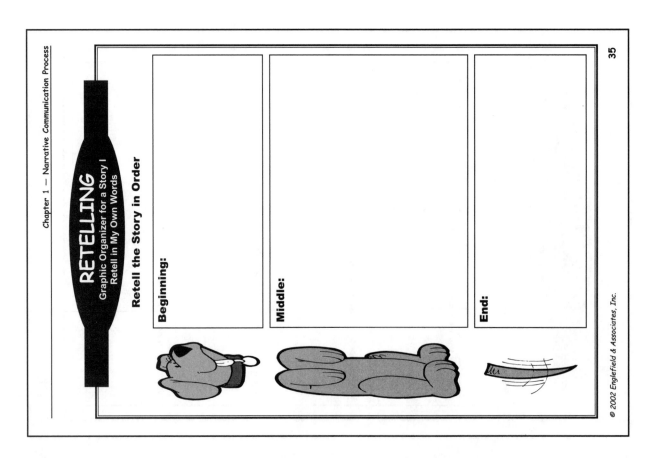

RETELLING
Graphic Organizer for a Story I
Retell in My Own Words

Retell the Story in Order

Beginning:

Middle:

End:

35

Writing Activity 6: Retelling
(A Story I Retell in My Own Words)

Step 1

Follow along as two passages are read. The first passage is a story titled "Rainy Day Picnic." The second passage is a retelling (a story I retell in my own words) of "Rainy Day Picnic."

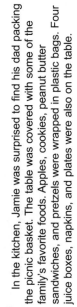

Rainy Day Picnic

Jamie had looked forward to this Saturday all week. His father said it was going to be Picnic Day. Jamie was sad when he looked out the window on Saturday morning. Rain was pouring from the sky. The clouds were dark. The trees moved with the blowing winds. "So much for Picnic Day," Jamie thought to himself.

In the kitchen, Jamie was surprised to find his dad packing the picnic basket. The table was covered with some of the family's favorite foods. Apples, cookies, peanut butter sandwiches, and pretzels were wrapped in plastic bags. Four juice boxes, napkins, and plates were also on the table.

"Where are we going on a rainy day?" Jamie asked.

"It's a surprise," said his dad. He finished packing the basket and closed the lid. "I know you will love it. Let's get going." When the family got in the car, Jamie's dad told him to close his eyes and keep them closed until he said, "We're here."

The family drove for a few minutes. Then, Jamie's dad stopped the car. "We're here," he said. Jamie opened his eyes. The car was parked in their own driveway. Everyone laughed. "I'm not letting rain ruin our Picnic Day," said Jamie's dad.

The family went inside. They spread a blanket on the floor. They ate the picnic lunch. Jamie's family told jokes and read books. Even though it was raining, everyone had a good time.

Step 6

The checklist shows what your best paper must have. Use the checklist below to review your work.

Checklist for Writing Activity 5

☐ My retelling starts with the beginning of the story.

☐ I use my own words to retell the story.

☐ My retelling includes the beginning, the middle, and the end.

☐ I use details from the story.

☐ My sentences end with a period, an exclamation point, or a question mark.

☐ My sentences begin with capital letters.

Step 3 *continued*

Hendrik's Mountain Adventure

In the mountains of a faraway place, there stands a sleepy little village called Vestorlennordland. The mountains are steep, and there are very few people who can find their way to the village. Of those who make the trip, almost none can say the name.

Hendrik Arvid is a young boy who lives in Vestorlennordland. His dream is to see the world outside the village. He plans and plans, and one day, he decides to start traveling. He packs a lunch of fish, yogurt, and cheese. After putting on a warm coat, he and his goat, Olaf, start their trip.

He walks down the mountain. He meets Mr. Gudrun. Mr. Gudrun is a woodcutter. "I'm going to see the world outside my village," Hendrik tells the woodcutter. Mr. Gudrun wishes Hendrik luck, and Hendrik keeps walking.

Hendrik walks up another mountain. He sees Mrs. Inger. She is gathering wild flowers. "I want to see the world," he tells her. She smiles and gives Olaf a pat on the head. Hendrik feels a little sad as he gets farther from his village.

Hendrik reaches a third mountain. Mr. Jorun is driving toward the village. "Where are you heading?" he asks Hendrik.

"Can you take me and Olaf back to the village?" asks Hendrik. He is happy when Mr. Jorun agrees. Although he wants to see distant places, he is most happy when he sees his own home.

Step 4

Answer the planning questions for the story you retell in your own words. Use your picture board or graphic organizer to help you think through your retelling (a story I retell in my own words). You can use pictures or words to plan your retelling (a story I retell in my own words).

40

Step 1 *continued*

Retelling of "Rainy Day Picnic"

Jamie woke up on Saturday. It was raining. He was sad because his family was supposed to go on a picnic. When Jamie went to the kitchen, he found his dad packing the picnic basket. All the family's favorite foods were on the table. Jamie's dad said they were going on the picnic, even though it was raining. They got in the car, and Jamie closed his eyes until the family got to the picnic place. When Jamie opened his eyes, they were at his house. The family had the picnic on a blanket in the house. They ate, shared stories, and had a good time.

Step 2

Remember, a good retelling (a story I retell in my own words) has the following parts.
• the title of the story
• my own words
• details from the story

Step 3

Use the following idea to plan your retelling (a story I retell in my own words).

Read the story titled "Hendrik's Mountain Adventure" on page 40. Retell the story so the reader will know all the important facts of the story.

39

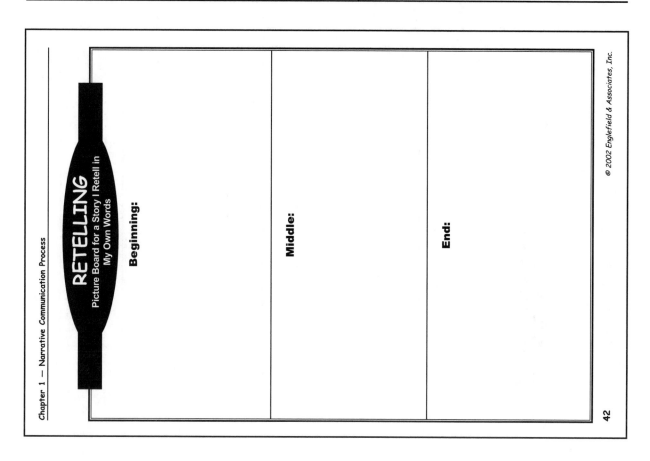

RETELLING

Picture Board for a Story I Retell in My Own Words

Beginning:

Middle:

End:

42

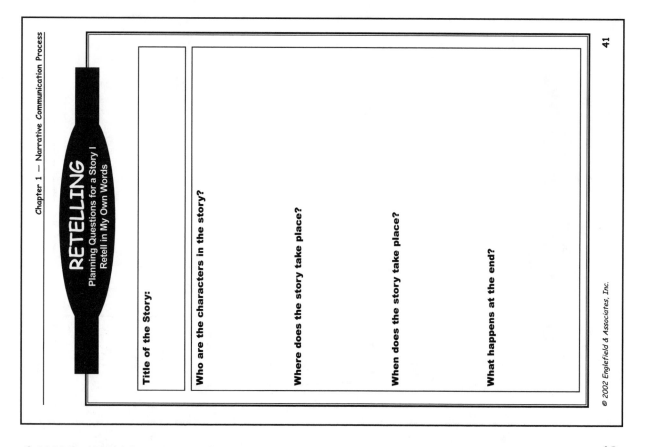

41

RETELLING

Planning Questions for a Story I Retell in My Own Words

Title of the Story:

Who are the characters in the story?

Where does the story take place?

When does the story take place?

What happens at the end?

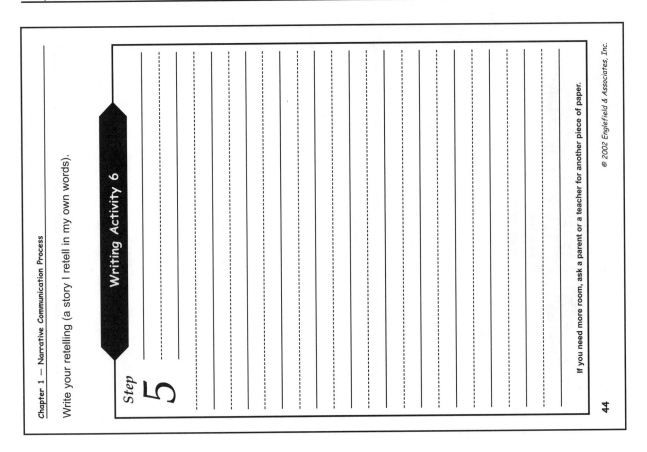

Step 6 The checklist shows what your best paper must have. Use the checklist below to review your work.

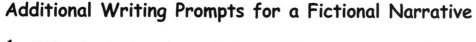

Checklist for Writing Activity 6

☐ My retelling starts with the beginning of the story.

☐ I use my own words to retell the story.

☐ My retelling includes the beginning, the middle, and the end.

☐ I use details from the story.

☐ My sentences end with a period, an exclamation point, or a question mark.

☐ My sentences begin with capital letters.

Additional Writing Prompts for a Fictional Narrative

1. Write about a hero in a tall tale or a fairy tale.

2. Write about a wacky invention that changed everything.

3. Create an unusual animal.

4. Give unusual abilities to an inanimate object, such as a shoe or a pencil, or write about a person with special powers or abilities.

5. Write a different beginning or ending to a story that was read aloud.

6. Write a story for a wordless picture book.

Additional Writing Prompts for a Personal Experience Narrative

1. Write about a time when you were happy or sad.

2. Write about a special place at home or at school.

3. Write about a time when you first tasted a food you either loved or disliked.

4. Write about a favorite person who is special to you.

5. Write about your favorite things.

6. Write about an event that you will never forget.

Additional Writing Prompts for a Retelling

1. Retell the story of "a first"—a first lost tooth, a first day at school, or a first time playing a sport.

2. Retell a predictable book or fairy tale.

3. Retell the story of a school morning— "When I got up . . ."

4. Retell the story of a book or a chapter that was read aloud to the class.

5. Retell a funny joke or story.

6. Retell a favorite television program or movie.

The Descriptive Communication Process
(Journal and Letter)

The purposes of this chapter include:

1 Showing how the descriptive communication process links to the writing modes.

2 Discussing the purpose and features of a letter and a journal.

3 Offering teaching tips on where students break down in the descriptive communication process.

4 Providing ideas for the development of additional writing prompts for journals and letters.

The following teaching tools are provided for a **journal**: planning questions, picture boards, graphic organizers, two writing prompts, and student checklists.

The following teaching tools are provided for a **letter**: planning guides, graphic organizers, two writing prompts, and student checklists.

What is the Descriptive Communication Process?

The purpose of description is to provide a mental picture of a person, a place, or a thing with vivid written details. Two examples of the descriptive communication process are the journal and the letter. Journals have been used and defined in a variety of ways—writer's notebooks, dialogue journals, personal journals or diaries, learning logs, and project journals. A journal can be written in paragraph or letter form. Some ideas to help students generate thoughts for a journal include: memories, hobbies, current events, questions, pets, plans, hopes, discoveries, and personal news.

Letters must be written in the proper form, including a date, a greeting, a body, a closing, and a signature. The topic will serve as the motivation for writing. Each letter will have a specific audience to address; however, an important thing to keep in mind is that the audience often varies from one letter to another.

Descriptions contain vivid sensory experiences and many specific details. The reader can imagine the person, the place, or the thing the writer describes. The written piece tells how the writer perceives the subject matter through as many senses as possible – sights, sounds, tastes, tactile sensations, and movement. A single person, place, or thing is often the major focal point for each descriptive section.

Features of a Journal
- Often the audience is oneself.
- The purpose is to record thoughts, feelings, and personal events.
- The format is often in paragraph form.
- The personal journal is often written in an informal style of writing.

> **Descriptive Communication information for students can be found on page 47 of the *Write on Target* Student Workbook.**

Features of a Letter
- The audience is specific, and the purpose is often a personal communication.
- Clearly addresses the audience with the intent to communicate
- Contains a date, a greeting, a body, a closing, and a signature
- Written with a very specific purpose

Correlation of Descriptive Communication to the Writing Modes

Below are the writing modes that reflect the importance of the descriptive communication process. The ability to describe is embedded in virtually all writing tasks and formats. Good writers describe so readers can experience what the authors want their audiences to experience. The journal and the letter were selected as the formats for students to practice and to refine their descriptive skills.

Journal – a piece of writing that includes a date and a description of the writer's feelings, or the sights, the sounds, the events, and the people the writer has encountered. Often, the audience is the writer.

Letter – a piece of writing that has a specific form, which includes a date, a greeting, a body, a closing, and a signature. A letter addresses a specific audience and establishes a written connection with that audience.

Teaching Tips:
Where Students Break Down in the Descriptive Communication Process

- Students do not use sufficient details to create the picture (image/scene).

- Students use unnecessary details to create the picture (image/scene).

- Students have a tendency to shift into other modes, especially narrative.

- Students want to tell the reader what to think about the person, the place, the thing, or the event, rather than showing the reader through vivid descriptions so the reader can form his or her own mental pictures. For example, a student may write, "*The girl was angry,*" rather than, "*The girl raised her clenched fist, and her face was red.*"

- In letter formats, students often do not establish a personal connection with the reader. Students omit either opening or closing comments. Examples of acceptable comments are listed below.

Sample opening comments:

Hope all is well with you.

I hope this letter finds you well.

I enjoyed your last visit (or letter).

Sample closing comments:

I look forward to seeing you.

Hope to see you soon.

Please write and tell me more about . . .

Writing Activity 7:
A Descriptive Journal

Step **1** Follow along as the December 10, 2002 journal entry is read.

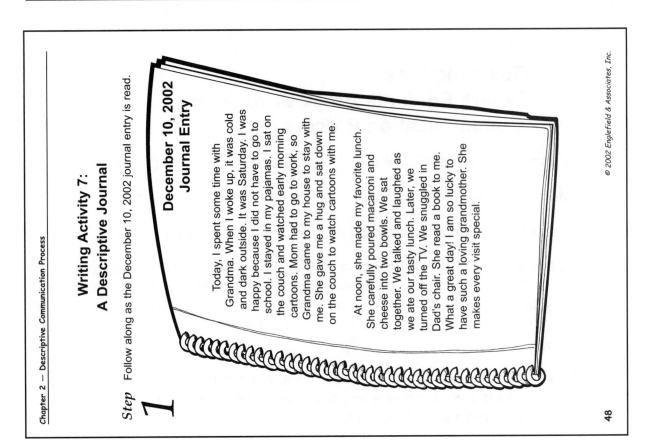

December 10, 2002 Journal Entry

Today, I spent some time with Grandma. When I woke up, it was cold and dark outside. It was Saturday. I was happy because I did not have to go to school. I stayed in my pajamas. I sat on the couch and watched early morning cartoons. Mom had to go to work, so Grandma came to my house to stay with me. She gave me a hug and sat down on the couch to watch cartoons with me.

At noon, she made my favorite lunch. She carefully poured macaroni and cheese into two bowls. We sat together. We talked and laughed as we ate our tasty lunch. Later, we turned off the TV. We snuggled in Dad's chair. She read a book to me. What a great day! I am so lucky to have such a loving grandmother. She makes every visit special.

48

Chapter 2

Description
(Journal and Letter)

What is Description?

The purpose of description is to create a picture. You should write descriptions when you want to let readers know how something looks, feels, sounds, tastes, or smells.

A journal is like a diary. You can record your thoughts and ideas in journals. Some things you may write about in journals include: memories, hobbies, pets, friends, family, and vacations.

A letter includes a date, a greeting, a body, a closing, and a signature. When you write a letter, you are writing to a particular person or group.

47

Page 50

JOURNAL ENTRY

Planning Questions for a Journal Entry

Use pictures or words.

Why are you writing about this day or time?

Who was there?

Where did it happen?

When did it happen?

What happened?

How did you feel?

50

Page 49

Step 2 Remember, a good journal entry has the following parts.
- a date
- a description of the day
- a description of your feelings
- a beginning, a middle, and an end

Step 3 Use the following idea to plan your journal entry.

> **Think about the part of your day that you like best. Date your journal and write about the best part of your day.**

Step 4 Answer the planning questions to get ideas for your journal. Use your picture board or graphic organizer to help you think through your journal entry. You can use pictures or words to plan your journal entry.

49

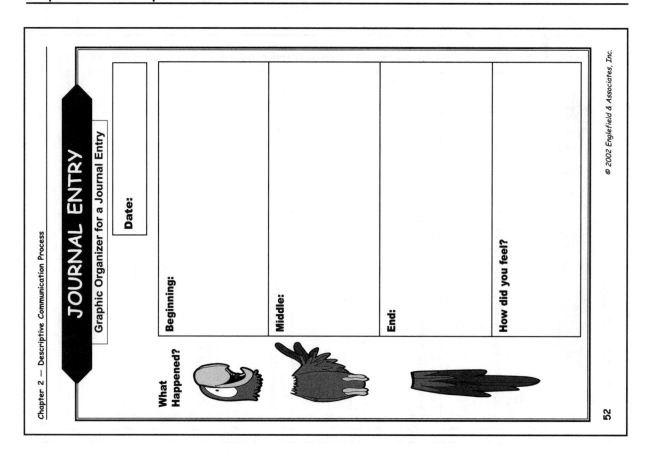

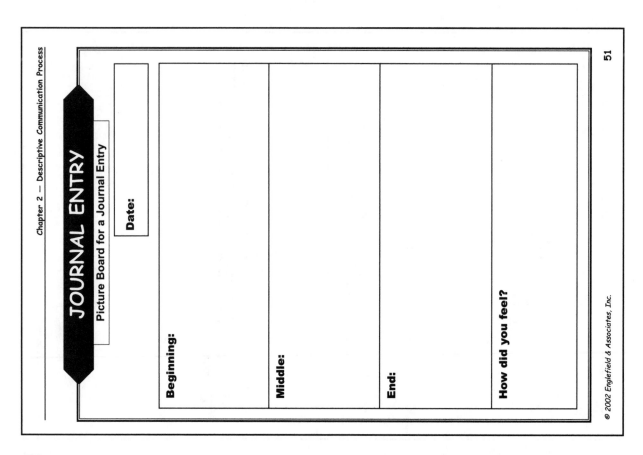

Step 6

The checklist shows what your best paper must have. Use the checklist below to review your work.

Checklist for Writing Activity 7

- ☐ My journal entry has a date.

- ☐ I describe people, places, things, and events from my day to make a picture.

- ☐ My journal entry has a beginning, a middle, and an end.

- ☐ I use words that tell what I heard, saw, and felt.

- ☐ My sentences end with a period, an exclamation point, or a question mark.

- ☐ My sentences begin with capital letters.

54

Writing Activity 7

Step 5

Write your journal entry.

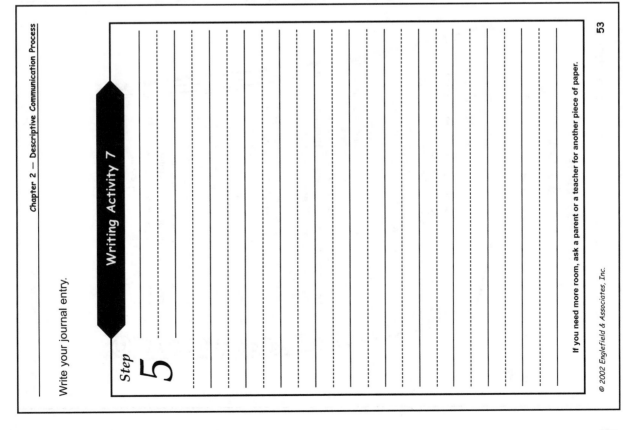

If you need more room, ask a parent or a teacher for another piece of paper.

53

Step

2

Remember, a good journal entry has the following parts.

- a date
- a description of the day
- a description of your feelings
- a beginning, a middle, and an end

Step

3

Use the following idea to plan your journal entry.

Think about a time you spent with a person or a pet you love. Describe what the person or the pet looks like, sounds like, and how the person or pet makes you feel.

Step

4

Answer the planning questions to get ideas for your journal. Use your picture board or graphic organizer to help you think through your journal entry. You can use pictures or words to plan your journal entry.

Writing Activity 8:
A Descriptive Journal

Step

1

Follow along as the July 4, 2002 journal entry is read.

July 4, 2002 Journal Entry

What a great day this has been! I have gone to parades before, but this Fourth of July parade was the best. My brother and I stood on the side of Main Street. We ate ice cream and waited for the parade to begin.

The parade started with a group of clowns. The clowns were dressed in brightly-colored outfits. They threw candy and passed out balloons. Next, a group of horses trotted down the street. They had shiny black coats. There were ribbons in their manes. A big red firetruck rolled behind the horses. The firefighters waved. When I heard a drumroll, I knew the marching band was coming. As they moved past me and my brother, the horns blew and the music started. The band was loud! There were many other sights, but I was most proud when I saw my uncle in the parade. He wore his policeman's uniform. He carried an American flag. I wanted everyone to know he was my uncle. He made the parade very special.

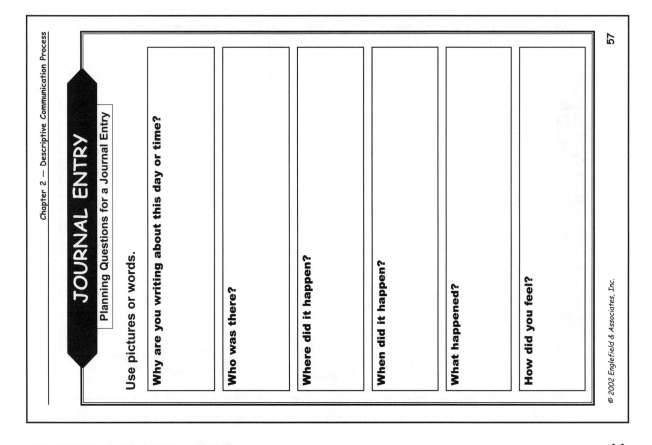

JOURNAL ENTRY

Picture Board for a Journal Entry

Date:

Beginning:

Middle:

End:

How did you feel?

58

57

JOURNAL ENTRY

Planning Questions for a Journal Entry

Use pictures or words.

Why are you writing about this day or time?

Who was there?

Where did it happen?

When did it happen?

What happened?

How did you feel?

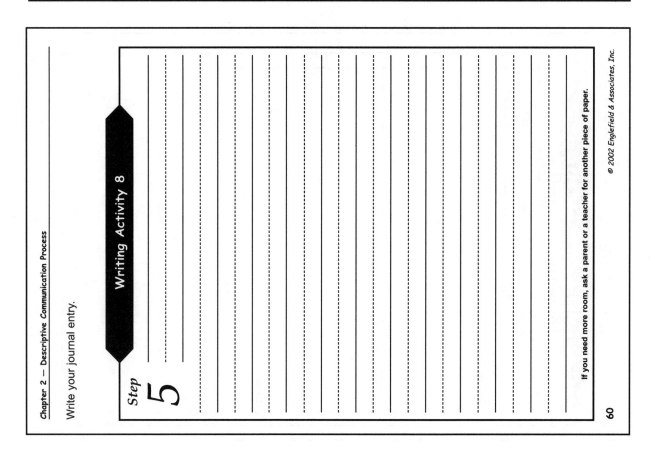

Write your journal entry.

Writing Activity 8

Step **5**

If you need more room, ask a parent or a teacher for another piece of paper.

60

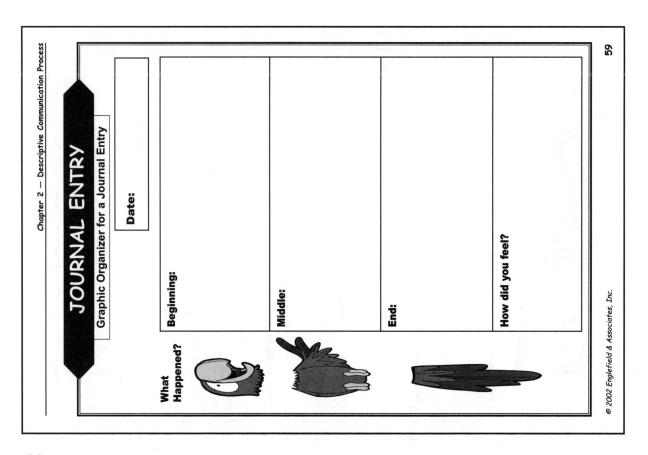

59

JOURNAL ENTRY

Graphic Organizer for a Journal Entry

Date:

What Happened?

Beginning:

Middle:

End:

How did you feel?

Writing Activity 9:
A Descriptive Letter

Step 1 Follow along as the descriptive letter is read aloud.

From Bill's Desk

March 16, 2002

Dear Bob,

I am glad you are here. I am writing to welcome you to the neighborhood. I heard your family just moved in. Mrs. Robinson told me she thinks you are about my age. I am seven.

Let me tell you about myself. I am in first grade. I go to Eastgate Elementary School. I like to play outside when the weather is warm. I really like to ride my bike. Sometimes, on summer evenings, the kids in the neighborhood catch lightning bugs. We put them in jars. I usually let mine go after an hour or so. Maybe you can join us sometime.

I hope we can meet soon. Write back and tell me about yourself.

Sincerely,

Bill

62

Step 6 The checklist shows what your best paper must have. Use the checklist below to review your work.

Checklist for Writing Activity 8

☐ My journal entry has a date.

☐ I describe people, places, things, and events from my day to make a picture.

☐ My journal entry has a beginning, a middle, and an end.

☐ I use words that tell what I heard, saw, and felt.

☐ My sentences end with a period, an exclamation point, or a question mark.

☐ My sentences begin with capital letters.

61

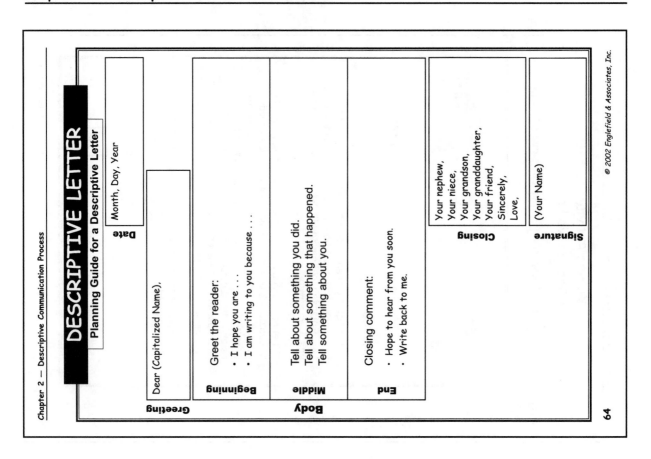

DESCRIPTIVE LETTER
Planning Guide for a Descriptive Letter

Greeting

Date: Month, Day, Year

Dear (Capitalized Name),

Body

Beginning

Greet the reader:
- I hope you are . . . .
- I am writing to you because . . .

Middle

Tell about something you did.
Tell about something that happened.
Tell something about you.

End

Closing comment:
- Hope to hear from you soon.
- Write back to me.

Closing

Your nephew,
Your niece,
Your grandson,
Your granddaughter,
Your friend,
Sincerely,
Love,

Signature

(Your Name)

64

Step **2**

Remember, a good descriptive letter has the following parts.
- a date
- a greeting
- a body that talks to the reader
- a closing
- a signature

Step **3**

Use the following idea to plan your descriptive letter.

> **Write a friendly letter to someone in your class. Write to someone who doesn't know you very well. Describe yourself so the reader knows who you are. Maybe the reader will want to meet you after reading your letter.**

Step **4**

Use the planning guide to get ideas for your letter. Use your graphic organizer to help you think through your descriptive letter. You can use pictures or words to plan your descriptive letter.

63

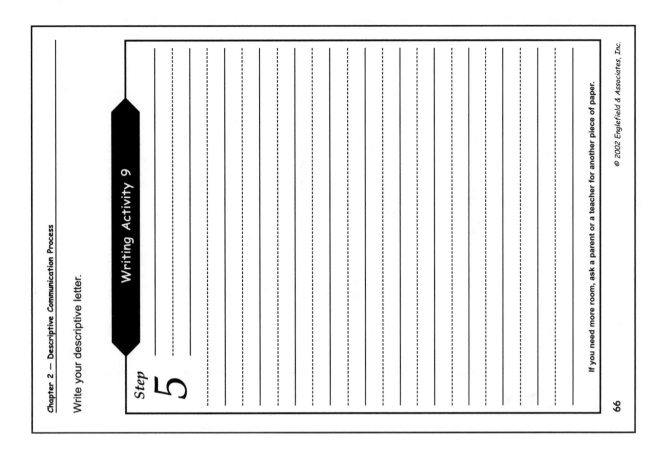

Write your descriptive letter.

Writing Activity 9

Step 5

66

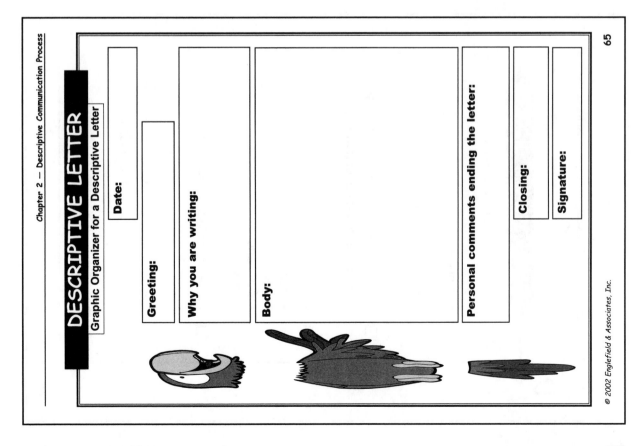

DESCRIPTIVE LETTER

Graphic Organizer for a Descriptive Letter

Date:

Greeting:

Why you are writing:

Body:

Personal comments ending the letter:

Closing:

Signature:

65

Writing Activity 10:
A Descriptive Letter

Step 1 Follow along as the descriptive letter is read aloud.

September 20, 2002

Dear Brandon,

I hope you are fine. I wanted to write you to let you know my new address. It is 8567 Woodview Drive. We just moved into our new house. I have my own room. My sister has her own room, too. There is plenty of room for me, my toys, and my two gerbils. I named one of the gerbils after you.

My new backyard has room for the swing set. This yard has a fence. Buddy runs and runs until he is so tired he cannot run anymore. My dad said he is going to plant a vegetable garden in one corner. It is a spot that gets a lot of sunlight. I hope I do not have to eat more vegetables. Even with the garden, there will be plenty of room to play soccer.

I have made a few new friends, but I miss everyone from our old neighborhood. I hope your mom will let you visit me soon. Write to me and tell me what is happening with you.

Your friend,

Brent

Step 6 The checklist shows what your best paper must have. Use the checklist below to review your work.

Checklist for Writing Activity 9

☐ I use the form for a letter, including:
- a date,
- a greeting,
- a body,
- a closing, and
- a signature.

☐ My letter tells my reader why I am writing and makes personal comments.

☐ I use words that help the reader:
- hear,
- see,
- feel, and
- think.

☐ My letter includes a personal closing comment.

☐ My sentences end with a period, an exclamation point, or a question mark.

☐ My sentences begin with capital letters.

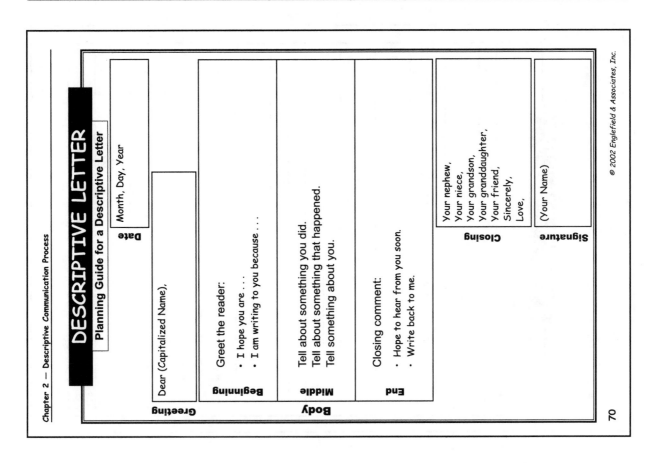

DESCRIPTIVE LETTER
Planning Guide for a Descriptive Letter

Date
Month, Day, Year

Greeting
Dear (Capitalized Name),

Body

Beginning
Greet the reader:
- I hope you are . . . .
- I am writing to you because . . . .

Middle
Tell about something you did.
Tell about something that happened.
Tell something about you.

End
Closing comment:
- Hope to hear from you soon.
- Write back to me.

Closing
Your nephew,
Your niece,
Your grandson,
Your granddaughter,
Your friend,
Sincerely,
Love,

Signature
(Your Name)

70

Step 2

Remember, a good descriptive letter has the following parts.
- a date
- a greeting
- a body that talks to the reader
- a closing
- a signature

Step 3

Use the following idea to plan your descriptive letter.

> **Write a friendly letter to a new pen pal. Describe your classroom. Use words that will help your pen pal see the classroom as you see it.**

Step 4

Use the planning guide to get ideas for your letter. Use your graphic organizer to help you think through your descriptive letter. You can use pictures or words to plan your descriptive letter.

69

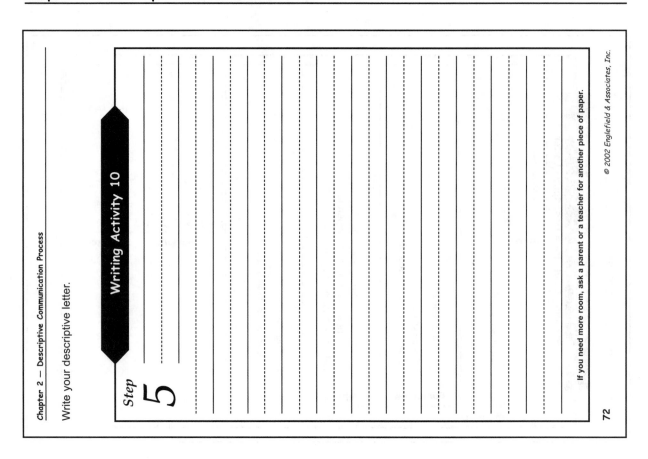

Write your descriptive letter.

Writing Activity 10

Step **5**

If you need more room, ask a parent or a teacher for another piece of paper.

© 2002 Englefield & Associates, Inc.

72

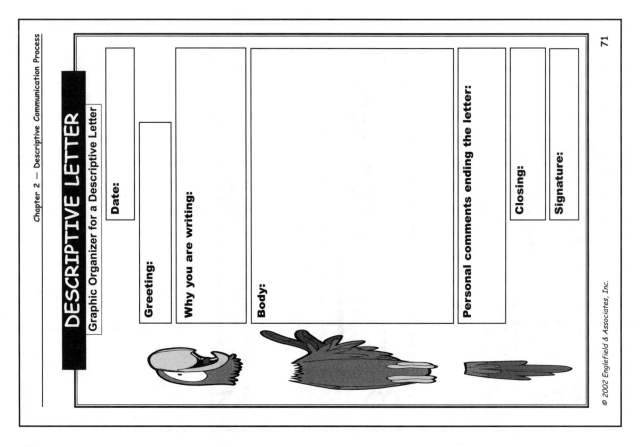

DESCRIPTIVE LETTER
Graphic Organizer for a Descriptive Letter

Date:

Greeting:

Why you are writing:

Body:

Personal comments ending the letter:

Closing:

Signature:

© 2002 Englefield & Associates, Inc.

71

Step 6

The checklist shows what your best paper must have. Use the checklist below to review your work.

Checklist for Writing Activity 10

☐ I use the form for a letter, including:
- a date,
- a greeting,
- a body,
- a closing, and
- a signature.

☐ My letter tells my reader why I am writing and makes personal comments.

☐ I use words that help the reader:
- hear,
- see,
- feel, and
- think.

☐ My letter includes a personal closing comment.

☐ My sentences end with a period, an exclamation point, or a question mark.

☐ My sentences begin with capital letters.

73

Additional Writing Prompts for a Journal Entry

1. Describe your favorite food or dessert.

2. Describe a place where you feel happy.

3. Describe yourself.

4. Describe a place in your school (classroom, cafeteria, gym) and tell what happens there.

5. Describe your favorite things to do when you are outside.

Additional Writing Prompts for a Descriptive Letter

1. Write a letter to someone new in your neighborhood introducing yourself or your family.

2. Write a letter to a friend who moved.

3. Write a letter to a famous person whom you like.

4. Write a letter to a grown-up who is nice to you.

5. Write a letter to a character in a book.

The Direction Communication Process
(Directions and Invitation)

The purposes of this chapter include:

1 Showing how the direction communication process links to the writing modes.

2 Discussing the purpose and the features of directions and of an invitation.

3 Offering teaching tips on where students break down in the direction communication process.

4 Providing ideas for the development of additional writing prompts for directions and an invitation.

> The following teaching tools are provided for **sets of directions** and an **invitation**: planning guides, graphic organizers, two writing prompts, and student checklists.

What is the Direction Communication Process?

The purpose of the direction communication process is to direct the reader to complete a set of actions that lead to a goal such as going somewhere or making something. Two examples of the direction communication process are directions and an invitation.

Features of Directions
- Provide communication that is orderly and efficient
- Assume the person who is being directed is not familiar with the task
- Written in correct chronological order or consecutive order
- Use words that provide directions

> Direction Communication information for students can be found on page 75 of the *Write on Target* Student Workbook.

Words that Provide Directions
- direction words: right, left, north, south, east, west
- prepositions: in, on, under, before, after
- adverbial phrases: when you see the . . . , before you reach the . . . , after you pass the . . .
- direction verbs: mix, blend, stir, insert, pour

Features of an Invitation
- Tells who is invited and who is hosting the event
- Indicates the type of event
- Indicates the time and the date of the event
- Indicates where the event will take place, and often includes a map to the location

Correlation of Direction Communication to the Writing Modes

Directions – a piece of writing that explains how to do something or how to go somewhere. It clearly describes the materials that are needed to complete the task and uses step-by-step order. Directions may be written in paragraph form or line by line. A starting point and an ending point are included.

Invitation – a piece of writing that can be in letter format. An invitation includes the purpose of the invitation, who is writing the invitation, who is being invited, where and when the event takes place, and any other important information.

Teaching Tips:
Where Students Break Down in the Direction Communication Process

- Students leave out information important to the completion of the task or goal because they assume that the listener knows what the student knows.

- Students provide more information than is necessary for the efficient completion of the task; they distract the reader with too much information.

- Students do not understand or do not use "direction words."

- Students switch into other communication modes, especially narrative.

- Students need to be able to visualize the directions they are going when using a map or a floor plan. Students need to picture themselves facing the direction they want to go to follow the steps. This may require turning the map or the floor plan.

Chapter 3

Directions
(Directions and Invitation)

What are Directions?

The purpose of directions is to tell someone how to make something or do something.

Directions

- can tell the reader how to make something, like a recipe.
- can tell the reader how to go somewhere, like a map.
- should be in step-by-step order.
- should be easy for the reader to follow.

An **invitation** is a short note or a letter that invites someone to an event such as a birthday party. Invitations include:

- what the event is,
- where the event is,
- the time of the event,
- the date of the event, and
- an RSVP (to tell them if you can come).

75

**Writing Activity 11: Directions
(How to Do Something)**

Step **1** Follow along as the directions on how to fix a bowl of cereal are read aloud.

How to Fix a Bowl of Cereal

To fix a bowl of cereal, you need a box of cereal, a bowl, a spoon, and some milk. First, pick the type of cereal you like to eat. Second, open the cereal box. Next, pour the cereal into a bowl. Then, open the milk container. Carefully pour the milk over the cereal. Don't pour too much milk into the bowl. If the bowl gets too full, the cereal will spill out. Finally, get your spoon and start to eat. You now know how to fix a bowl of cereal, so crunch away and enjoy your cereal.

76

DIRECTIONS

Planning Guide for How To Do Something

How To:

WORDS YOU COULD USE IN YOUR DIRECTIONS:

Order words

first	second	third
next	then	finally

Prepositions

in	under	after	behind
on	before	over	beneath
around	next to	near	

Doing verbs

mix	stir
blend	insert

Sentence starters

First, you will . . . .
Then, you should . . . .
Finally, you will . . . .

78

Step **2** Remember, good directions have the following parts.

- a beginning that tells the reader what the directions will explain how to do
- a description of what is needed to complete the task
- steps that are given in order
- a starting point and an ending point

Step **3** Use the following idea to plan your directions.

> **Your friend loves chocolate milk but has never made it. Write directions for your friend. After reading your directions, your friend should be able to make chocolate milk.**

Step **4** Use the planning guide to get ideas for your directions. Use your graphic organizer to help you think through your directions. You can use pictures or words to plan your directions.

77

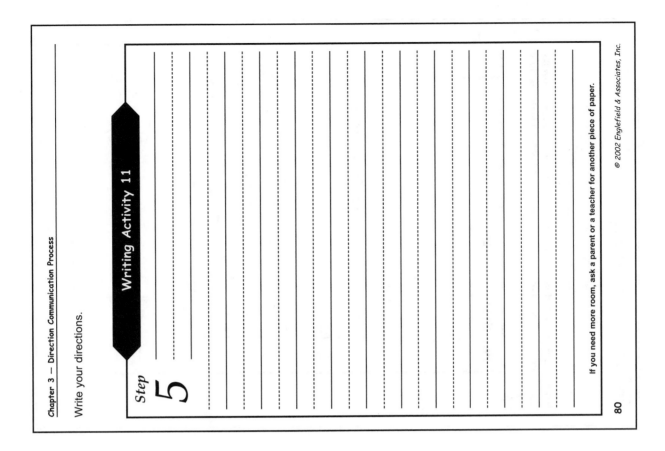

Write your directions.

Writing Activity 11

Step

5

If you need more room, ask a parent or a teacher for another piece of paper.

80

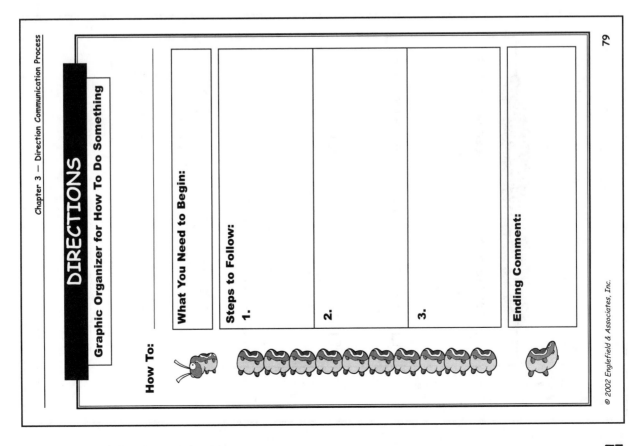

DIRECTIONS

Graphic Organizer for How To Do Something

How To:

What You Need to Begin:

Steps to Follow:

1.

2.

3.

Ending Comment:

79

Writing Activity 12: Directions
(How to Go Somewhere)

Step
1

Look at the picture below. Follow along in your booklets now as the set of directions on how to get to the toy section of the store are read aloud.

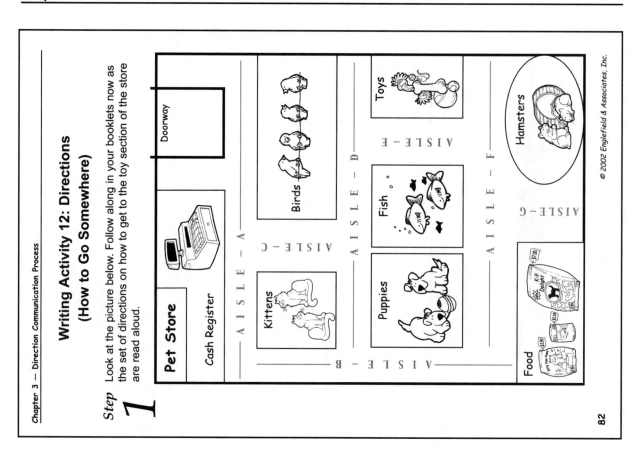

82

Step
6

The checklist shows what your best paper must have. Use the checklist below to review your work.

◗ Checklist for Writing Activity 11

☐ My directions begin with a sentence that tells what my directions will explain how to do.

☐ I tell what materials are needed to begin the task.

☐ I use the correct order to tell the reader what steps to follow.

☐ I include an ending comment describing the completed task.

☐ My sentences end with a period, an exclamation point, or a question mark.

☐ My sentences begin with capital letters.

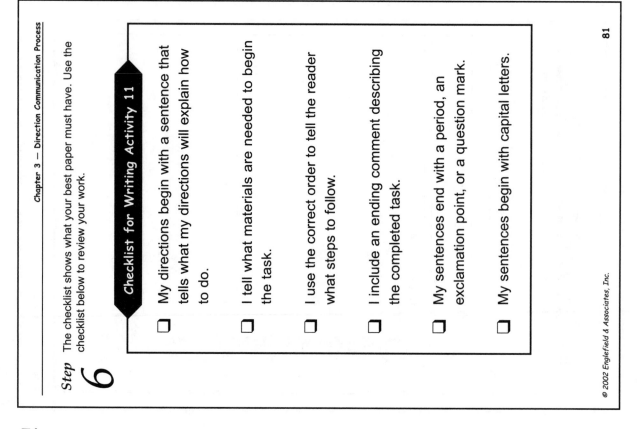

81

Step 3 *continued*

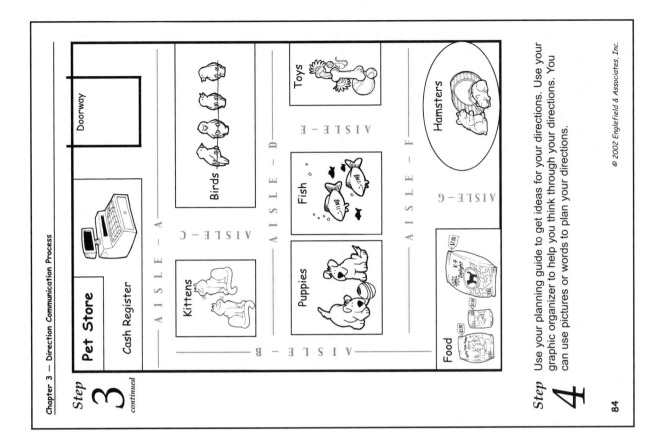

Pet Store

Cash Register

AISLE - A

AISLE - B

AISLE - C

AISLE - D

AISLE - E

AISLE - F

AISLE - G

Kittens

Puppies

Birds

Fish

Toys

Hamsters

Food

Doorway

Step 4 Use your planning guide to get ideas for your directions. Use your graphic organizer to help you think through your directions. You can use pictures or words to plan your directions.

84

Step 1 *continued*

When you give directions, you have to picture yourself facing the direction you want to go as you follow the steps.

Your friend wants to buy a toy for a new pet. Turn the pet store map and pretend you are entering the door. Give your friend directions to the toy section.

1. When you walk into the store, you will see the cash register on your right and the birds in front of you.

2. Turn right and walk down Aisle A.

3. When you see the kittens, turn left and walk down Aisle C.

4. When you see the puppies and the fish in front of you, turn left and walk down Aisle D.

5. Go to the end of Aisle D and the toys will be on your right.

6. Select the toy your friend's pet will enjoy the most!

* Note: There is more than one way to give directions to the toy section.

Step 2 Remember, good directions have the following parts.

- a beginning that tells the reader what the directions will explain how to do
- a description of what is needed to complete the task
- steps that are given in order
- a starting point and an ending point

Step 3 Use the following idea to plan your directions.

Your friend is in aisle E and is looking at the toys. Write directions for your friend. Tell your friend how to get from the toy section to the door.

83

DIRECTIONS

Graphic Organizer for How To Go Somewhere

How To:

Where you are going:

Where to start:

Steps to Follow:

1.

2.

3.

Where you will end up:

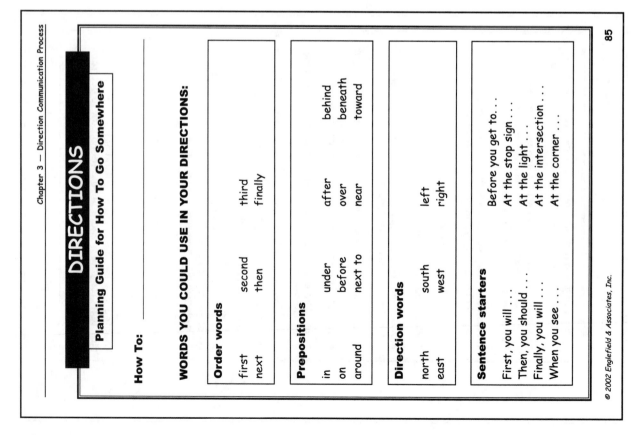

86

DIRECTIONS

Planning Guide for How To Go Somewhere

How To:

WORDS YOU COULD USE IN YOUR DIRECTIONS:

Order words

first	second	third
next	then	finally

Prepositions

in	under	after	behind
on	before	over	beneath
around	next to	near	toward

Direction words

north	south	left
east	west	right

Sentence starters

First, you will . . .   Before you get to . . .
Then, you should . . . .   At the stop sign . . .
Finally, you will . . . .   At the light . . . .
When you see . . . .   At the intersection . . . .
                              At the corner . . . .

85

Step 6

The checklist shows what your best paper must have. Use the checklist below to review your work.

Checklist for Writing Activity 12

☐ My directions begin with a sentence that tells where my directions will take the reader.

☐ I tell where to start.

☐ I give the directions in the correct order to get to the location.

☐ I include an ending comment telling where the reader will end.

☐ My sentences end with a period, an exclamation point, or a question mark.

☐ My sentences begin with capital letters.

88

Write your directions.

Step 5

Writing Activity 12

_____

_____

_____

_____

_____

_____

_____

_____

_____

_____

_____

_____

_____

If you need more room, ask a parent or a teacher for another piece of paper.

87

Step **2**

Remember, a good invitation has the following parts.

- information about where and when to attend
- the purpose of the event
- information for an RSVP
- all important details about the event

Step **3**

Use the following idea to plan your invitation.

You are going to have a party. Write an invitation to your friends so they will know why you are having the party.

Step **4**

Use your planning guide to get ideas for your invitation. Use your graphic organizer to help you think through your invitation. You can use pictures or words to plan your invitation.

90

Writing Activity 13:
Invitation

Step **1**

Follow along as the invitation is read aloud.

September 25, 2002

Dear Bart,

My birthday is almost here, and I'm having a party. You are invited to come to my birthday party on October 12, 2002. I live at 6298 Brownstone Court. The party will begin at 2:00 p.m. It will end at 4:00 p.m. We will play games and eat cake. We will have lots of fun. Call 555-5555 by October 5th to let me know if you can come. I hope to see you there.

Sincerely,

Lori

89

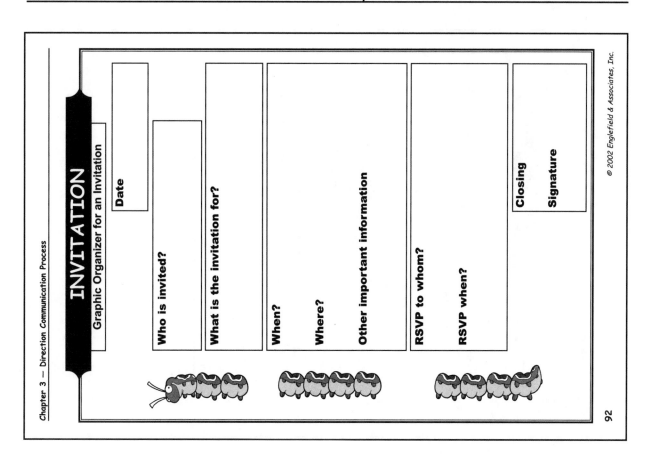

INVITATION
Graphic Organizer for an Invitation

Date

Who is invited?

What is the invitation for?

When?

Where?

Other important information

RSVP to whom?

RSVP when?

Closing

Signature

© 2002 Englefield & Associates, Inc.

92

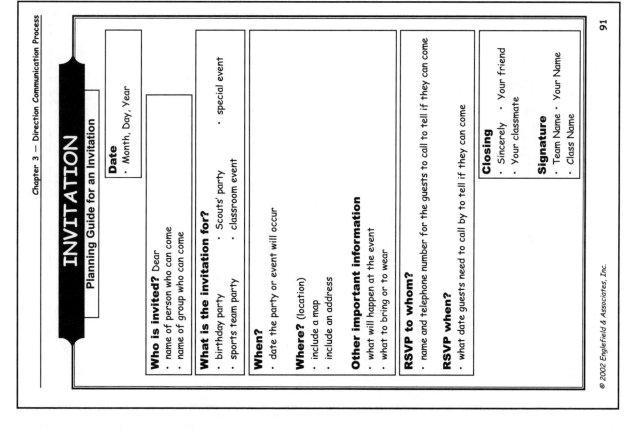

INVITATION
Planning Guide for an Invitation

Date
· Month, Day, Year

Who is invited? Dear
· name of person who can come
· name of group who can come

What is the invitation for?
· birthday party   · Scouts' party   · special event
· sports team party   · classroom event

When?
· date the party or event will occur

Where? (location)
· include a map
· include an address

Other important information
· what will happen at the event
· what to bring or to wear

RSVP to whom?
· name and telephone number for the guests to call to tell if they can come

RSVP when?
· what date guests need to call by to tell if they can come

Closing
· Sincerely   · Your friend
· Your classmate

Signature
· Team Name · Your Name
· Class Name

91

© 2002 Englefield & Associates, Inc.

Chapter 3 — Direction Communication Process

The checklist shows what your best paper must have. Use the checklist below to review your work.

Step 6

Checklist for Writing Activity 13

☐ My invitation includes all the important details for my guest, such as:
- what the invitation is for,
- when to attend,
- who is invited,
- RSVP information (for guests to tell if they can come), and
- a closing with a name or a signature.

☐ My sentences end with a period, an exclamation point, or a question mark.

☐ My sentences begin with capital letters.

© 2002 Englefield & Associates, Inc.

94

Chapter 3 — Direction Communication Process

Write your invitation.

Step 5

Writing Activity 13

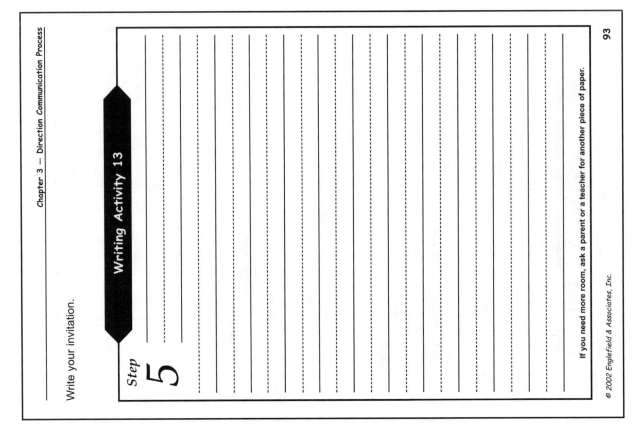

If you need more room, ask a parent or a teacher for another piece of paper.

© 2002 Englefield & Associates, Inc.

93

Step 2

Remember, a good invitation has the following parts.

- information about where and when to attend
- the purpose of the event
- information for an RSVP
- all important details about the event

Step 3

Use the following idea to plan your invitation.

> Your class is having a party for people who volunteer in your classroom. Write an invitation. Invite the volunteers to this special party.

Step 4

Use your planning guide to get ideas for your invitation. Use your graphic organizer to help you think through your invitation. You can use pictures or words to plan your invitation.

96

Writing Activity 14: Invitation

Step 1

Follow along as the invitation is read aloud.

December 1, 2002

Dear Grandpa,

I am writing to invite you to a holiday concert at my school. The concert will be held at New Hope Elementary School on December 20, 2002. The concert starts at 9:00 a.m. and ends at 10:00 a.m. After the concert, you are invited to stay for cookies and punch. We will be singing many holiday songs. You are welcome to sing along, if you would like. I would really like to see you there. I hope you can make it. Please check your calendar and RSVP by December 13th by calling 333-3333.

Love,

Blake

95

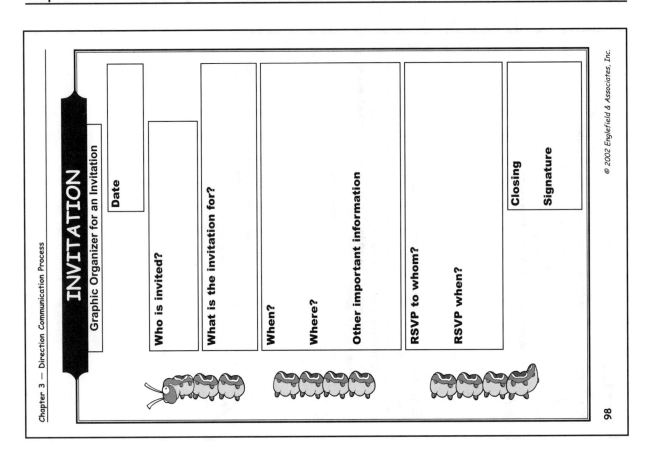

INVITATION
Graphic Organizer for an Invitation

Date

Who is invited?

What is the invitation for?

When?

Where?

Other important information

RSVP to whom?

RSVP when?

Closing

Signature

98

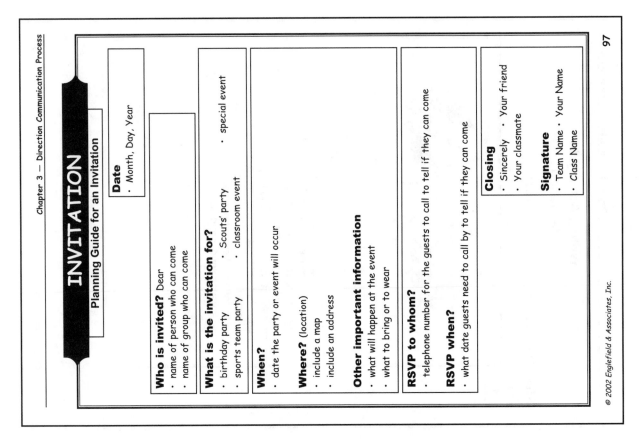

INVITATION
Planning Guide for an Invitation

Date
· Month, Day, Year

Who is invited? Dear
· name of person who can come
· name of group who can come

What is the invitation for?
· birthday party   · Scouts' party   · special event
· sports team party   · classroom event

When?
· date the party or event will occur

Where? (location)
· include a map
· include an address

Other important information
· what will happen at the event
· what to bring or to wear

RSVP to whom?
· telephone number for the guests to call to tell if they can come

RSVP when?
· what date guests need to call by to tell if they can come

Closing
· Sincerely   · Your friend
· Your classmate

Signature
· Team Name · Your Name
· Class Name

97

The checklist shows what your best paper must have. Use the checklist below to review your work.

Step **6**

Checklist for Writing Activity 14

☐ My invitation includes all the important details for my guest, such as:

- what the invitation is for,
- when to attend,
- who is invited,
- RSVP information (for guests to tell if they can come), and
- a closing with a name or a signature.

☐ My sentences end with a period, an exclamation point, or a question mark.

☐ My sentences begin with capital letters.

Write your invitation.

Step **5**

Writing Activity 14

If you need more room, ask a parent or a teacher for another piece of paper.

Additional Writing Prompts for Directions on How to Do Something

1. how to make a phone call

2. how to put on a band-aid

3. how to wash your hands

4. how to put on a piece of clothing

5. how to play your favorite game

6. how to make your favorite sandwich

7. how to clean a window

8. how to carve a pumpkin

9. how to make your favorite ice cream cone or sundae

10. how to vacuum the floor

Additional Prompts for Directions on How to Go Somewhere or How to Find Something

1. directions to complete an Easter egg hunt

2. directions to find an object hidden in the room or the school

3. directions from your classroom to the principal's office, playground, gym, or lunchroom

4. directions to find a location on a map

Additional Writing Prompts for Writing an Invitation to:

1. a cookout

2. a school event

3. an awards event

4. a family gathering (reunion)

5. a party

6. a movie

7. a sleepover

8. a volunteer appreciation event

The Explanation Communication Process
(Informational Report, Summary, and Thank-You Note)

The purposes of this chapter include:

1 Showing how the explanation communication process links to the writing modes.

2 Discussing the purpose and features of an informational report, a summary, and a thank-you note.

3 Providing teaching tips on where students break down during the explanation communication process.

4 Providing ideas for the development of additional writing prompts for an informational report, a summary, and a thank-you note.

The following teaching tools are provided for an **informational report**: planning questions, a graphic organizer, two writing prompts, and student checklists.

The following teaching tools are provided for a **summary** and a **thank-you note**: a planning guide, a graphic organizer, two writing prompts, and student checklists.

What is the Explanation Communication Process?

Explanation is a communication process that appears across all subject areas in the curriculum. The purpose of explanation is for the writer to give reasons why something occurred.

For an explanation, the writer gives a reason or an opinion with a justification; he or she must be able to provide facts with supporting details. An explanation may require the ability to infer (*e.g.*, Why do you think the character felt that way?). Oftentimes, an explanation requires the ability to use only information given in a selection to support the explanation. Understanding cause and effect is important to the explanation process (*e.g.*, This happened because . . .).

Features of an Informational Report

- Nonfiction writing about a person, place, thing, or event.
- Provides information about some or all of the following questions.

What or who is it?	Where is it?
What does it look like?	When is it?
What does it do?	Why is it important?

Explanation Communication information for students can be found on page 101 of the *Write on Target* Student Workbook.

Features of a Summary (Only the Important Information)

- The main idea is identified.
- Supporting details are not included.
- Trivial and redundant information is not included.
- Similar facts, ideas, and information are grouped across paragraphs.
- Only the information essential to complete the communication is conveyed.
- The summary is shorter in length than the original.
- A summary is told in the student's own words.

Features of the Thank-You Note

- Written in letter format with date, greeting, body, closing, and signature
- Explains why the writer is thankful for something done for or given to him or her

---

Correlation of Explanation Communication to the Writing Modes

Informational – a piece of nonfiction writing that is based on researched facts but is written in the student's own words. It is presented in an organized format with a beginning, a middle, and an end. It can be a report and can cover a wide variety of topics. The purpose of an informational piece of writing is to inform the reader about what the author has learned.

Summary – a piece of writing identifying what the text selection is about. A summary states the main ideas of the text selection. It does not include information that is not important. A summary has fewer details than a retelling.

Thank-You Note – a piece of writing that is written in the form of a letter and includes a date, a greeting, a body, a closing, and a signature. A thank-you note explains what the writer is thankful for and why.

Teaching Tips:
Where Students Break Down in the Explanation Communication Process

In general, students have difficulty:
- Understanding when to infer and when to use the selection to make their points. (Example: Students are asked to use ONLY the text selection to provide evidence for their opinions or statements, or students are asked to explain their own opinions, conclusions, or observations based on the information provided in the text.)
- Understanding the relationship between cause and effect.
- Using facts and supporting details (when necessary).
- Distinguishing between facts and opinions in the selection.

Informational Report
- Students have difficulty organizing the information in a logical order.
- Students do not provide a closing to the report. The closing should summarize the importance of the ideas presented.
- Some students are unable to pick out the important ideas and eliminate nonessential information.
- Some students have difficulty writing the ideas in their own words.

Summary
- Students have difficulty picking out the main idea, especially in paragraphs that do not have topic sentences.
- Students have difficulty eliminating nonessential information.
- Students have difficulty using titles, subheadings, and boldface words to compose their summaries.

Thank-You Note
- Students do not address the reader with an appropriate greeting.
- Students have difficulty explaining or expressing why the gift or the favor was appreciated.

Writing Activity 15: Informational Report

Step **1** Follow along as the informational report "Rabbits" is read aloud.

Rabbits

Rabbits are mammals. They have fur that is soft and thick. They have short, fuzzy tails and long ears. Rabbits use their strong back legs and feet to run and to hop.

Rabbits like to eat plants, flowers, grass, clover, and vegetables. Many times, rabbits will eat from people's gardens. This causes some people to think rabbits are pests.

Rabbits live near fields, shrubs, and grassy places. Rabbits make their homes in underground holes or in shrubs. These homes provide shelter.

You can see rabbits any time of day. However, rabbits are most active during the early evening and at night. Be careful; if you scare them, the only things you will see are their fuzzy tails as they dart away!

Next time you are outside, keep your eye out for these mammals. Are the rabbits you see cute creatures or harmful pests?

Explanation
(Informational Report, Summary, and Thank-You Note)

What is Explanation?

Writers give an explanation when they want readers to understand something. An explanation uses facts or details.

An **informational report** contains facts. Reports can be written on real people, places, things, or events. An informational report is nonfiction.

A **summary** is short. A summary gives only the main ideas; it does not contain details. A summary should be written in your own words.

A **thank-you note** is a short note thanking someone for something that was given to you or done for you. A thank-you note is written in the form of a letter; it includes a date, a greeting, a body, a closing, and a signature.

Step
3
continued

Emergency Medical Technicians

- Emergency medical technicians are called EMTs.
- EMTs work in fire departments.
- EMTs take people to the hospital.
- EMTs put bandages on cuts.
- EMTs go to car crashes and fires.
- Gloves help EMTs stay safe and healthy.
- EMTs give medical care to people during an emergency.
- EMTs treat people who are sick.
- EMTs put splints on broken bones.
- EMTs help people who are hurt.
- EMTs give oxygen to people who cannot breathe.
- EMTs wear sterile gloves.
- EMTs save lives.
- EMTs drive ambulances.
- EMTs use backboards to carry people who are hurt.

Step
4

Use your planning questions and your graphic organizer to help you think through your informational report. You can use pictures or words to plan your informational report.

© 2002 Englefield & Associates, Inc.

104

Step
2

Remember, an informational report has the following parts.
- a title
- a sentence telling what the report is about
- important information about the topic
- details about what I have learned about the topic
- a summary that ends the report

Step
3

Use the following idea to plan your informational report.

Read through the information given about emergency medical technicians on the next page. Use the planning questions on page 105 to gather information. Use the information you gather in the planning questions to complete your graphic organizer.

You do not have to use every fact to complete your informational report. You will need to organize the material and add words of your own.

Write an informational report about emergency medical technicians using the facts given. Use the graphic organizer to write an introduction, a paragraph, and a summary that ends your report.

© 2002 Englefield & Associates, Inc.

103

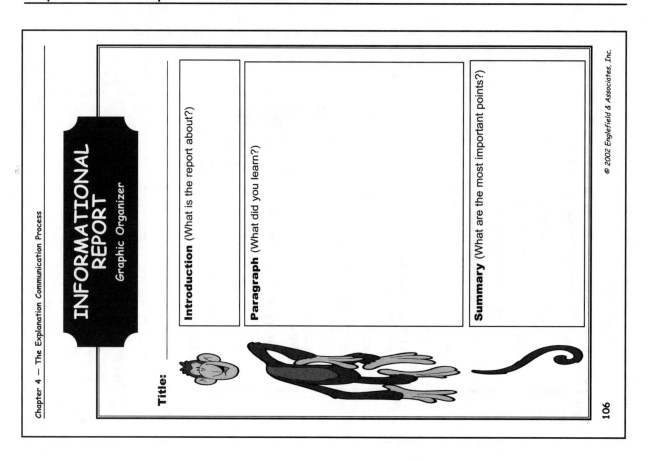

INFORMATIONAL REPORT
Graphic Organizer

Title:

Introduction (What is the report about?)

Paragraph (What did you learn?)

Summary (What are the most important points?)

106

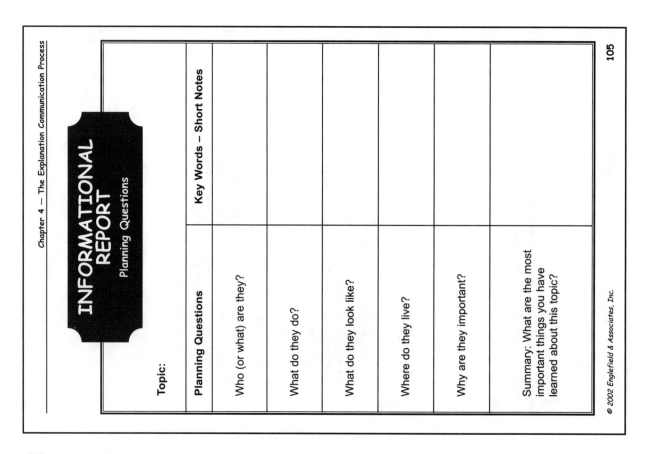

INFORMATIONAL REPORT
Planning Questions

Topic:

Planning Questions	Key Words – Short Notes
Who (or what) are they?	
What do they do?	
What do they look like?	
Where do they live?	
Why are they important?	
Summary: What are the most important things you have learned about this topic?	

105

Step 6

The checklist shows what your best paper must have. Use the checklist below to review your work.

Checklist for Writing Activity 15

☐ My informational report has a title.

☐ My informational report has a beginning that tells the reader what my report is about.

☐ My informational report has a paragraph that tells the reader what I have learned.

☐ My informational report includes a summary of the most important parts.

☐ My sentences end with a period, an exclamation point, or a question mark.

☐ My sentences begin with capital letters.

© 2002 Englefield & Associates, Inc.

108

Write your informational report.

Step 5

Writing Activity 15

© 2002 Englefield & Associates, Inc.

If you need more room, ask a parent or a teacher for another piece of paper.

107

Step
2

Remember, an informational report has the following parts.

- a title
- a sentence telling what the report is about
- important information about the topic
- details about what I have learned about the topic
- a summary that ends the report

Step
3

Use the following idea to plan your informational report.

Read through the information given about wolves on the next page. Use the planning questions on page 112 to gather information. Use the information you gather in the planning questions to complete your graphic organizer.

You do not have to use every fact to complete your informational report. You will need to organize the material and add words of your own.

Write an informational report about wolves using the facts given. Use the graphic organizer to write an introduction, a paragraph, and a summary that ends your report.

Writing Activity 16:
Informational Report

Step
1

Follow along as the informational report "Wind" is read aloud.

Wind

Wind is moving air. We cannot see wind, but we can see wind move things. We can see wind push clouds across the sky or rustle the leaves on trees. Wind can carry a kite high toward the sky. It can blow wind chimes, which make pretty sounds. Wind can move a sailboat across the water. Wind carries the seeds of plants to new places where they can take root and grow. These are good things about wind.

Sometimes, when wind is strong, it can cause damage. Strong wind can knock over trees and telephone poles. Strong wind can cause objects to fly through the air and break things. If the ground is dry, strong wind can blow away topsoil.

Wind can be gentle or strong. On warm days, wind causes air to move. This cools us down and feels good against our skin. Other times, wind can blow very hard. This type of wind can cause damage. Sometimes wind helps us, but sometimes it does not.

INFORMATIONAL REPORT
Planning Questions

Topic:

Planning Questions	Key Words – Short Notes
Who (or what) are they?	
What do they do?	
What do they look like?	
Where do they live?	
Why are they important?	
Summary: What are the most important things you have learned about this topic?	

112

Step

3
continued

Wolves

- Wolves live in many different places.
- A wolf is a type of wild dog.
- Each wolf pack has a leader.
- A group of wolves is called a pack.
- Wolves look for food and water together.
- A wolf can have as many as 11 pups at a time.
- Sometimes wolves live in dens.
- A baby wolf is called a pup.
- Wolves are like dogs.
- Wolves do many things in packs.
- Wolves hunt many kinds of animals.
- A den may be a cave or a hollow log.
- Wolves grow thick fur in the winter.
- The other wolves follow the leader of the pack.
- Wolves share their food with the pack.
- Wolf pups are born in the winter.
- Sometimes dens are underground.
- Wolves can bark, growl, and howl.
- The adult wolves take care of their young pups.
- Dogs are better pets than wolves.
- Wolves are wild animals.

Step

4

Use your planning questions and your graphic organizer to help you think through your informational report. You can use pictures or words to plan your informational report.

111

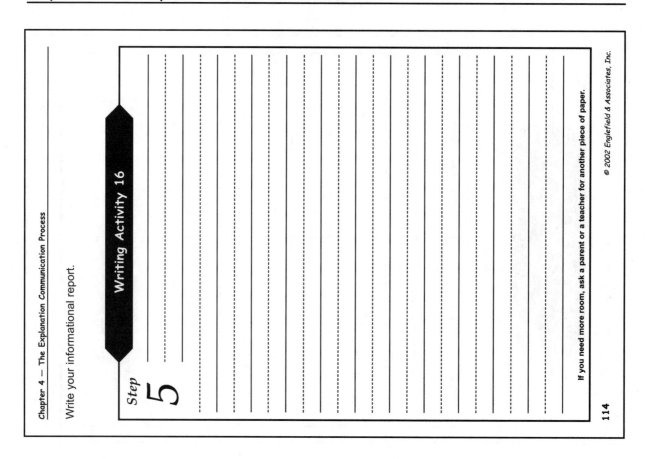

Write your informational report.

Writing Activity 16

Step **5**

If you need more room, ask a parent or a teacher for another piece of paper.

© 2002 Englefield & Associates, Inc.

114

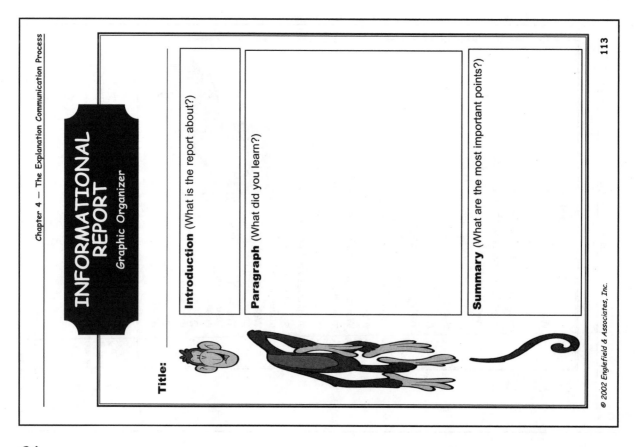

© 2002 Englefield & Associates, Inc.

113

INFORMATIONAL REPORT
Graphic Organizer

Title:

Introduction (What is the report about?)

Paragraph (What did you learn?)

Summary (What are the most important points?)

Writing Activity 17: Summary
(Only the Main Ideas)

Step
1

Follow along as two passages are read aloud. The first passage is a report titled "George Washington Carver." The second passage is a summary of "George Washington Carver."

George Washington Carver

George Washington Carver was born in 1864 in Missouri. He lived and worked on the Moses Plantation until he was ten years old. His work on the plantation helped George develop his love of the outdoors and science. He left the plantation to move to another town so he could go to school.

George is best known for his work with peanuts. He developed over 300 uses for the peanut. He also developed many uses for soybeans, pecans, and sweet potatoes. You might recognize some of the things he helped develop. Some of the things he made using peanuts include buttermilk, chili sauce, glue, ink, instant coffee, laundry soap, mayonnaise, metal polish, paint, paper, plastic, shampoo, shaving cream, shoe polish, talcum powder, and wood stain.

As you can see, George Washington Carver's many inventions are important in our lives today. If it were not for his work, things might be very different. George was one of the greatest inventors of all time!

116

Step
6

The checklist shows what your best paper must have. Use the checklist below to review your work.

Checklist for Writing Activity 16

☐ My informational report has a title.

☐ My informational report has a beginning that tells the reader what my report is about.

☐ My informational report has a paragraph that tells the reader what I have learned.

☐ My informational report includes a summary of the most important parts.

☐ My sentences end with a period, an exclamation point, or a question mark.

☐ My sentences begin with capital letters.

115

Step 3 *continued*

Parrots

Parrots are brightly colored birds. They usually live in places where the weather is warm and wet. Many types of parrots have green feathers. Parrots with green feathers are the most common. Parrots can also have blue, yellow, red, purple, pink, brown, or black feathers.

Parrots have four toes. Two of their toes point forward. Two of their toes are turned backward. This makes them walk strangely, but they are great climbers. They use their toes and their bills to help them move from branch to branch.

Parrots eat mostly seeds and fruits. They like to build their nests in holes found in the ground, in trees, or in rocks.

Parrots are very smart. Some parrots make noises that sound like human voices. This is why some people like to have parrots as pets. There is one thing you should know: if you buy a parrot just to hear it talk, you might be unhappy. Only a small number of parrots ever learn to talk.

by Lainie Burke

Step 4 Use your planning guide and graphic organizer to help you think through your summary (only the main ideas). You can use pictures or words to plan your summary (only the main ideas).

118

Step 1 *continued*

Summary of "George Washington Carver"

George Washington Carver was from Missouri. He was born in 1864. He lived on the Moses Plantation. He loved nature and science. He developed many uses for the peanut. He invented many things we still use today. George Washington Carver was a great inventor.

Step 2 Remember, a good summary (only the main ideas) has the following parts.

- main ideas
- no unimportant or unnecessary information
- a small amount of detail
- my own words

Step 3 Use the following idea to plan your summary (only the main ideas).

Read the report titled "Parrots" on page 118. Write a summary (only the main ideas).

117

Page 120

STEPS FOR WRITING A SUMMARY

Graphic Organizer Including Only the Main Ideas

Topic:

Write what the text selection is about. Include only important information.

Beginning:

Main Idea:

Ending:

120

Page 119

STEPS FOR WRITING A SUMMARY

Planning Guide for Including Only the Main Ideas

Topic:

Complete the Following Steps:

Step 1 ☐ Skim the reading selection and begin to look for the main idea.

Step 2 ☐ Underline the topic sentence for each paragraph in the text selection. (If there is no topic sentence, write one for the paragraph.)

Step 3 ☐ Cross out unimportant information in the text selection.

Step 4 ☐ Cross out information that is repeated.

119

Step 6

The checklist shows what your best paper must have. Use the checklist below to review your work.

Checklist for Writing Activity 17

☐ My summary includes only important information.

☐ My summary starts at the beginning.

☐ My summary states the main idea.

☐ My summary has an ending.

☐ My summary does not include information that is not important.

☐ My sentences end with a period, an exclamation point, or a question mark.

☐ My sentences begin with capital letters.

122

Write your summary.

Writing Activity 17

Step 5

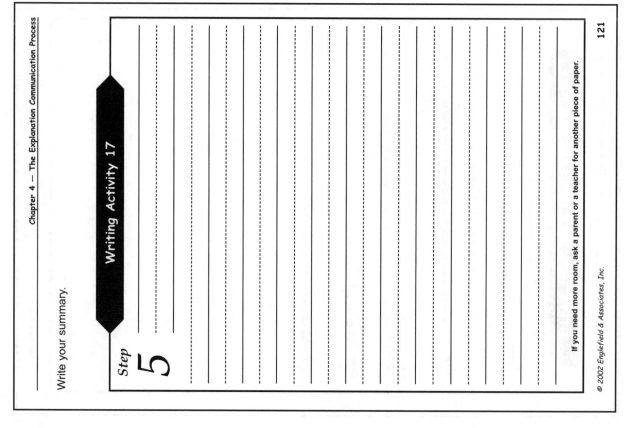

If you need more room, ask a parent or a teacher for another piece of paper.

121

Page 124

Step 1 *continued*

Summary of "Fighting Fires"

Firefighters put out big fires. An alarm lets them know when it's time to go to a fire. They go to fires in their trucks. The trucks have hoses and ladders. Firefighters use water to put out fires. They connect their hoses to special trucks and to fire hydrants. This is where the water comes from. When firefighters get to a fire, they put out the fire and help save people. Firefighters are brave. Their job is important.

Step 2 Remember, a good summary (only the main ideas) has the following parts.

- main ideas
- no unimportant or unnecessary information
- a small amount of detail
- my own words

Step 3 Use the following idea to plan your summary (only the main ideas).

Read the report titled "Frogs" on page 125. Write a summary (only the main ideas).

Page 123

Writing Activity 18: Summary (Only the Main Ideas)

Step 1 Follow along as two passages are read aloud. The first passage is a report titled "Fighting Fires." The second passage is a summary of "Fighting Fires."

Fighting Fires

Firefighters are called when there is a fire that is too big to be put out by other people. When people call to say they need a fire put out, an alarm goes off at the fire station. This alarm lets the firefighters know they need to get in their trucks and go to the fire.

Fire trucks are not like normal trucks. You have probably seen one before. They are long and red. They carry hoses and ladders. There is also a special truck that holds a large tank of water. Firefighters use the tank of water to start putting out a fire. Other firefighters look for fire hydrants. Fire hydrants can be found on streets and near buildings. The fire hydrants are connected to pipes that hold water. Firefighters hook their hoses to the hydrants. Then, they turn on the hydrants. Water shoots through the hoses and helps firefighters put out fires.

When the firefighters get to a fire, the firefighter who is in charge looks around to see what is happening. Then, he tells the other firefighters what they need to do. Some put out the fire, and others might have to help rescue people. Firefighters are very brave people. Fire fighting is an important job that helps keep people safe.

by Lainie Burke

STEPS FOR WRITING A SUMMARY

Planning Guide for Including Only the Main Ideas

Topic:

Complete the Following Steps:

Step 1 ☐ **Skim the reading selection and begin to look for the main idea.**

Step 2 ☐ **Underline the topic sentence for each paragraph in the text selection.** (If there is no topic sentence, write one for the paragraph.)

Step 3 ☐ **Cross out unimportant information in the text selection.**

Step 4 ☐ **Cross out information that is repeated.**

126

Step 3 *continued*

Frogs

Frogs live both in water and on land. They have to stay near fresh water. They cannot survive in salt water. Frogs are good swimmers and jumpers. They have long, muscular back legs to help them jump. Most frogs have four webbed feet. These help them swim.

Frogs are coldblooded. This means their body temperatures are the same as the air temperature around them. They have to look for cool, shady places to rest if they become too hot. Frogs look for warm, sunny places if they are too cold.

Frogs have backbones. Their eyes bulge out from their faces. They can see in most directions without turning their heads. The skin of a frog is smooth and slightly damp. Frogs have teeth in their upper jaws and no teeth in their lower jaws. Frogs use their long, sticky tongues to catch bugs. They swallow their food whole.

Step 4 Use your planning guide and graphic organizer to help you think through your summary (only the main ideas). You can use pictures or words to plan your summary (only the main ideas).

125

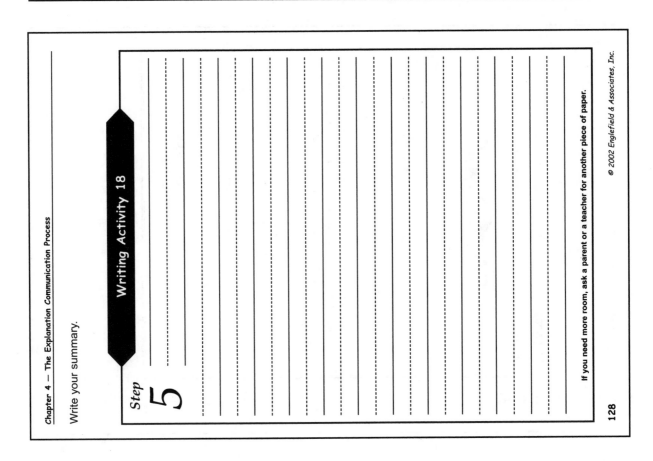

Write your summary.

Writing Activity 18

Step **5**

If you need more room, ask a parent or a teacher for another piece of paper.

128

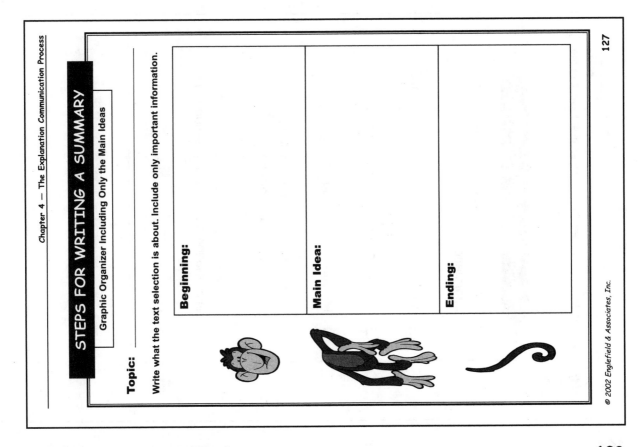

STEPS FOR WRITING A SUMMARY

Graphic Organizer Including Only the Main Ideas

Topic:

Write what the text selection is about. Include only important information.

Beginning:

Main Idea:

Ending:

127

Writing Activity 19: Thank-You Note

Step 1 Follow along as the thank-you note is read aloud.

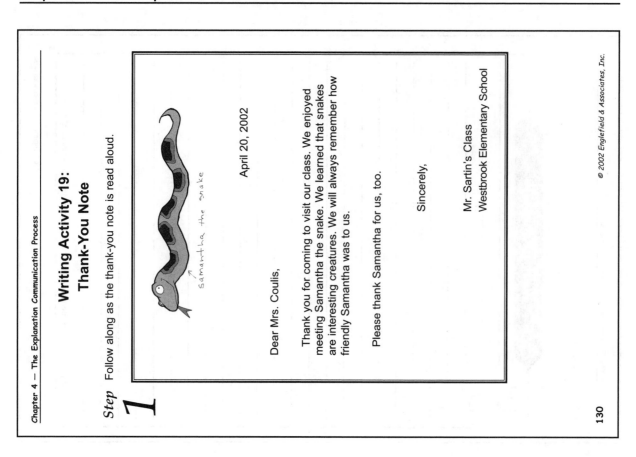

Samantha the snake

April 20, 2002

Dear Mrs. Coulis,

Thank you for coming to visit our class. We enjoyed meeting Samantha the snake. We learned that snakes are interesting creatures. We will always remember how friendly Samantha was to us.

Please thank Samantha for us, too.

Sincerely,

Mr. Sartin's Class
Westbrook Elementary School

130

Step 6 The checklist shows what your best paper must have. Use the checklist below to review your work.

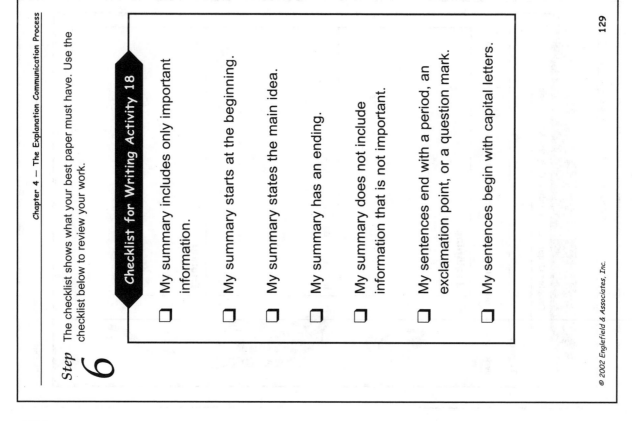

Checklist for Writing Activity 18

☐ My summary includes only important information.

☐ My summary starts at the beginning.

☐ My summary states the main idea.

☐ My summary has an ending.

☐ My summary does not include information that is not important.

☐ My sentences end with a period, an exclamation point, or a question mark.

☐ My sentences begin with capital letters.

129

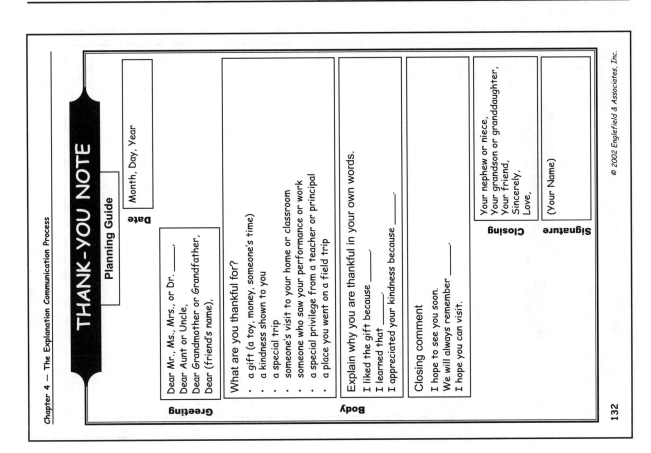

Step

2

Remember, a good thank-you note has the following parts.

- the date
- a greeting
- a body
- a closing
- a signature

Step

3

Use the following idea to plan your thank-you note.

You received a special gift. Write a thank-you note to the person who gave you the gift. Explain why you are thankful.

Step

4

Use your planning guide and graphic organizer to help you think through your thank-you note. You can use pictures or words to plan your thank-you note.

131

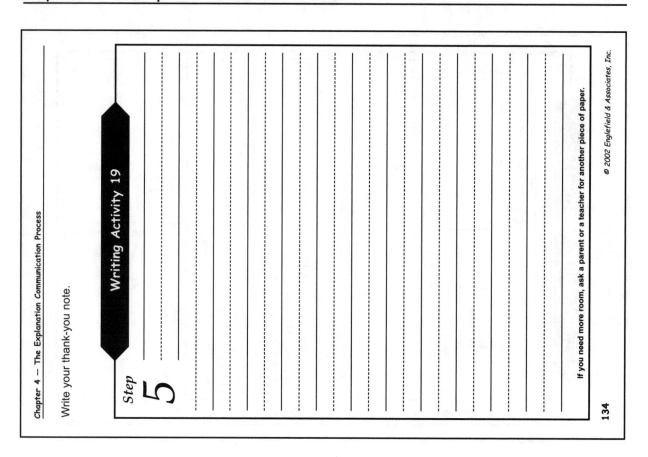

Chapter 4 — The Explanation Communication Process

Write your thank-you note.

Writing Activity 19

Step **5**

If you need more room, ask a parent or a teacher for another piece of paper.

134

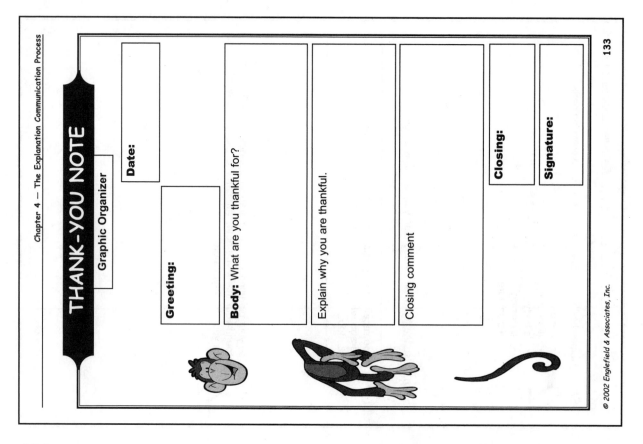

Chapter 4 — The Explanation Communication Process

THANK-YOU NOTE

Graphic Organizer

Date:

Greeting:

Body: What are you thankful for?

Explain why you are thankful.

Closing comment

Closing:

Signature:

133

Page 136

Writing Activity 20: Thank-You Note

Step 1

Follow along as the thank-you note is read aloud.

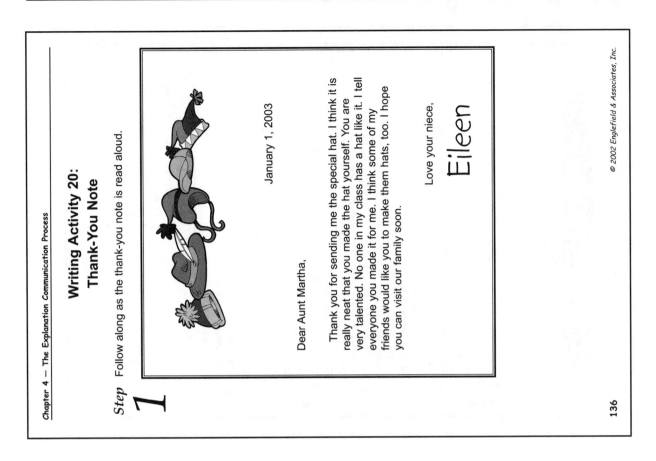

January 1, 2003

Dear Aunt Martha,

Thank you for sending me the special hat. I think it is really neat that you made the hat yourself. You are very talented. No one in my class has a hat like it. I tell everyone you made it for me. I think some of my friends would like you to make them hats, too. I hope you can visit our family soon.

Love your niece,

Eileen

136

Page 135

Step 6

The checklist shows what your best paper must have. Use the checklist below to review your work.

Checklist for Writing Activity 19

☐ I use the form for a letter.

☐ My thank-you note tells my reader what I am thankful for.

☐ My thank-you note explains why I am thankful.

☐ My thank-you note includes an ending.

☐ I try to spell words correctly.

☐ My sentences end with a period, an exclamation point, or a question mark.

☐ My sentences begin with capital letters.

135

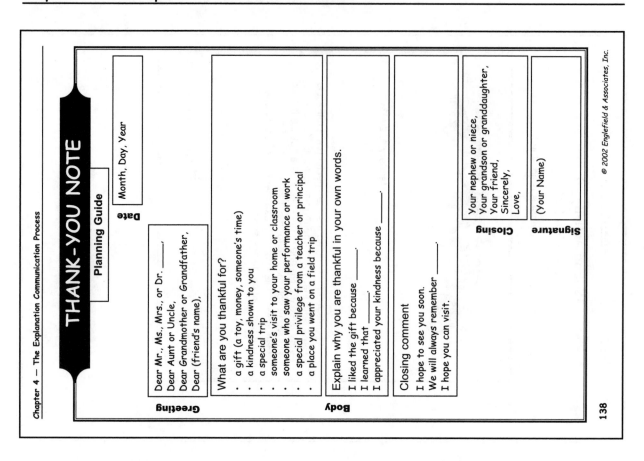

THANK-YOU NOTE

Planning Guide

Date
Month, Day, Year

Greeting
Dear Mr., Ms., Mrs., or Dr. _____,
Dear Aunt or Uncle,
Dear Grandmother or Grandfather,
Dear (friend's name).

Body

What are you thankful for?
- a gift (a toy, money, someone's time)
- a kindness shown to you
- a special trip
- someone's visit to your home or classroom
- someone who saw your performance or work
- a special privilege from a teacher or principal
- a place you went on a field trip

Explain why you are thankful in your own words.
I liked the gift because _____.
I learned that _____.
I appreciated your kindness because _____.

Closing comment
I hope to see you soon.
We will always remember _____.
I hope you can visit.

Closing
Your nephew or niece,
Your grandson or granddaughter,
Your friend,
Sincerely,
Love,

Signature
(Your Name)

138

Step **2**
Remember, a good thank-you note has the following parts.
- the date
- a greeting
- a body
- a closing
- a signature

Step **3**
Use the following idea to plan your thank-you note.

Write a thank-you note to someone in your school for something special he or she taught you or did for you. Some people you may want to consider thanking include a teacher, a principal, a bus driver, a custodian, a fellow student, a parent volunteer, or a cafeteria worker.

Step **4**
Use your planning guide and graphic organizer to help you think through your thank-you note. You can use pictures or words to plan your thank-you note.

137

108

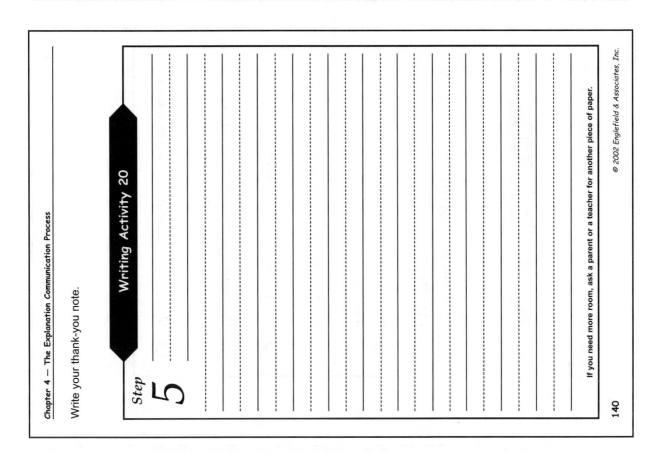

Write your thank-you note.

Writing Activity 20

Step **5**

If you need more room, ask a parent or a teacher for another piece of paper.

140

© 2002 Englefield & Associates, Inc.

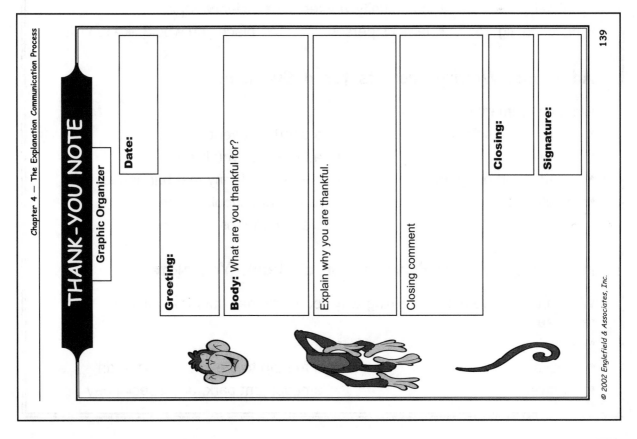

Chapter 4 — The Explanation Communication Process

THANK-YOU NOTE

Graphic Organizer

Date:

Greeting:

Body: What are you thankful for?

Explain why you are thankful.

Closing comment

Closing:

Signature:

139

© 2002 Englefield & Associates, Inc.

Step 6

The checklist shows what your best paper must have. Use the checklist below to review your work.

Checklist for Writing Activity 20

☐ I use the form for a letter.

☐ My thank-you note tells my reader what I am thankful for.

☐ My thank-you note explains why I am thankful.

☐ My thank-you note includes an ending.

☐ I try to spell words correctly.

☐ My sentences end with a period, an exclamation point, or a question mark.

☐ My sentences begin with capital letters.

© 2002 Englefield & Associates, Inc.

141

Additional Writing Prompts for an Informational Report

Write a report on a(n):
- animal
- community worker
- science topic
- historical figure
- famous person
- place you would like to visit

Additional Writing Prompts for a Summary

Write a summary of:
- your day at school
- a movie
- a television program
- a field trip
- a sporting event
- a book that you liked
- something funny that happened to you at school, on the playground, or on the bus

Additional Writing Prompts for a Thank-You Note

Write a thank-you note explaining why you were thankful for a gift you received:
- clothing
- books
- software
- toys
- a fun trip to the zoo, a visit to an amusement park, or a special day

The Persuasive Communication Process
(Persuasive Letter)

The purposes of this chapter include:

1 Showing how the persuasive communication process links to the writing modes.

2 Discussing the purpose and features of a persuasive letter.

3 Offering teaching tips on where students break down in the persuasive communication process.

4 Providing ideas for the development of additional writing prompts for persuasive letters.

> The following teaching tools are provided for a **persuasive letter**: a planning guide, a graphic organizer, two writing prompts, and a student checklist.

What is the Persuasive Communication Process?

The purpose of persuasion is to influence another person's or group's thinking about a particular issue. Persuasive techniques can be observed in letters to the editor, advertising campaigns, and speeches.

Features of a Persuasive Letter

- The writer must state his or her position on an issue.
- The writer must provide supporting evidence or reasons for the position taken.
- The reasons should be logical and based on facts (not opinion).
- The writer must anticipate and acknowledge the "other side's" point of view.

> Persuasive Communication information for students can be found on page 143 of the *Write on Target* Student Workbook.

Language of Persuasion

It is my belief that . . .	On the other hand . . .	What is your point?
In my opinion . . .	State	However . . .
As noted . . .	Opinion	Yet . . .
As you can see . . .	I see your point.	I doubt . . .
In conclusion . . .	For these reasons . . .	Argue
Pro	Point of view	Con

Correlation of Persuasive Communication to a Writing Mode

Persuasive Letter – a piece of writing that is written in the form of a letter and includes a date, a greeting, a body, a closing, and a signature. A persuasive letter expresses the writer's opinion and why it is important by using facts, examples, or reasons. It also states what the writer would like to see happen.

Teaching Tips:
Where Students Break Down in the Persuasive Communication Process

- Students do not understand the difference between fact and opinion.

- Students fail to recognize that there can be a variety of possible positions; there is rarely one "right" position.

- The reasons that students give to influence somebody else's thinking are based on just personal opinion, not facts.

- Students do not have enough information to argue a position.

Writing Activity 21:
Persuasive Letter

Step

1

Follow along as the persuasive letter is read aloud.

September 13, 2002

Dear Mr. Williams,

I think students should be able to bring drinks to school. As you know, we do not have air conditioning, and our school can be very hot. On hot days, students get very thirsty. Our teachers give us drinking fountain breaks. Sometimes we get thirsty in between these breaks. If we could have drinks in class, we would not have to worry about breaks.

Not all students like water. If they brought their own drinks, they could bring what they like. If we all brought our own drinks, we would not have to worry about germs. My mom told me there are germs on the drinking fountain. When students stay away from germs, they do not get sick as often.

Please change the school rule. Let students bring drinks to school. This way, we will not be thirsty on hot days.

Sincerely,

Sophie Ruiz

Chapter 5

Persuasion
(Persuasive Letter)

What is Persuasion?
The purpose of persuasion is to change how the reader thinks or feels about something. One way to persuade someone is to write a persuasive letter.

A **persuasive letter** is written to an editor of a newspaper, a teacher, a principal, a parent, or anyone else you want to persuade. Persuasive letters include information you want readers to know about. Often, these letters are written when you want to convince others about how you think or feel.

- You tell your thoughts and feelings.
- You give reasons.
- You tell them what you want to have happen.

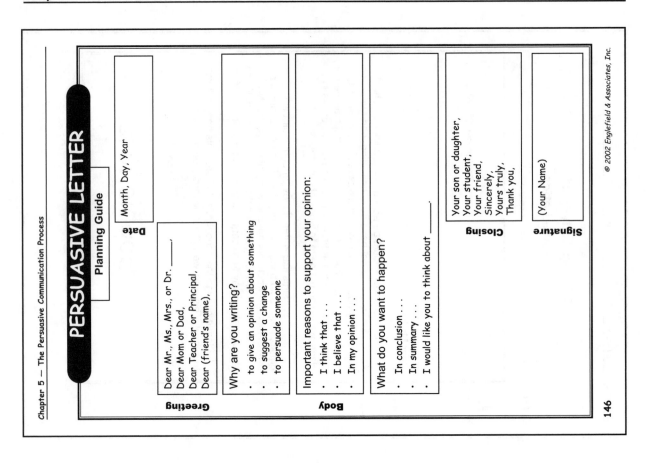

PERSUASIVE LETTER

Planning Guide

Date
Month, Day, Year

Greeting
Dear Mr., Ms., Mrs., or Dr. _____,
Dear Mom or Dad,
Dear Teacher or Principal,
Dear (friend's name),

Body

Why are you writing?
- to give an opinion about something
- to suggest a change
- to persuade someone

Important reasons to support your opinion:
- I think that . . .
- I believe that . . .
- In my opinion . . .

What do you want to happen?
- In conclusion . . . .
- In summary . . . .
- I would like you to think about _____

Closing
Your son or daughter,
Your student,
Your friend,
Sincerely,
Yours truly,
Thank you,

Signature
(Your Name)

146

© 2002 Englefield & Associates, Inc.

Step 2
Remember, a good persuasive letter has the following parts.
- a date, a greeting, a body, a closing, and a signature
- a statement of your opinion
- facts that support your opinion
- a conclusion that restates your opinion

Step 3
Use the following idea to plan your persuasive letter.

Write a persuasive letter to your principal about something you think needs to be changed in your school.

Step 4
Use your planning guide and graphic organizer to help you think through your persuasive letter. You can use pictures or words to plan your persuasive letter.

145

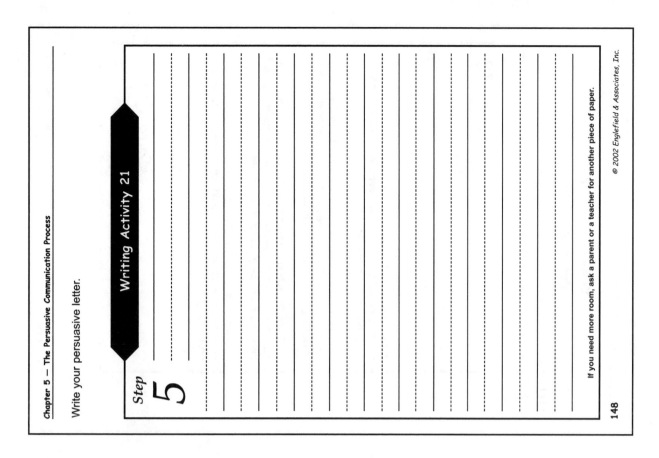

Write your persuasive letter.

Writing Activity 21

Step 5

If you need more room, ask a parent or a teacher for another piece of paper.

© 2002 Englefield & Associates, Inc.

148

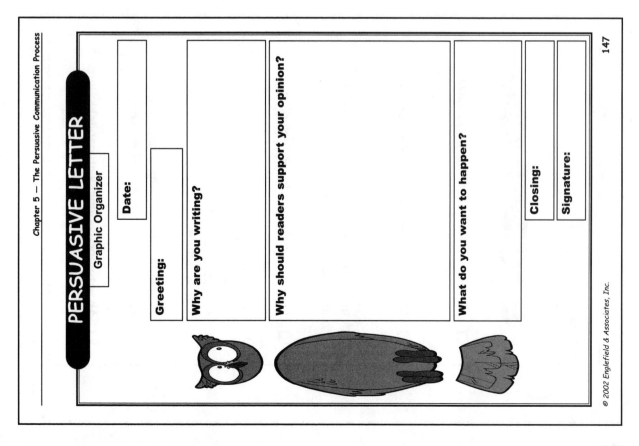

PERSUASIVE LETTER

Graphic Organizer

Date:

Greeting:

Why are you writing?

Why should readers support your opinion?

What do you want to happen?

Closing:

Signature:

© 2002 Englefield & Associates, Inc.

147

Writing Activity 22:
Persuasive Letter

Step
1

Follow along as the persuasive letter is read aloud.

April 15, 2002

Dear Ms. Peters,

I am writing to tell you I believe the school library needs to stay open during the summer months. There is no library in our neighborhood. Many children have no way to get to the library on the other side of town.

If our school library were open, children would have something to do. Reading helps us learn. Right now, instead of learning, many kids get into trouble.

Since the school is in our neighborhood, we could walk to the school library. We would have no problem getting there. I think this would be good for all kids in the area.

Please talk to the people in charge of the school library. Let them know the students would like it if the library were open during the summer months.

Sincerely,

Keith Clark

Step
6

The checklist shows what your best paper must have. Use the checklist below to review your work.

Checklist for Writing Activity 21

☐ I tell what I am writing my persuasive letter about.

☐ My letter gives reasons why I believe my opinion is important.

☐ In my conclusion, I say what I would like to happen.

☐ I use the form for a letter, including:
   - a date,
   - a greeting,
   - a body,
   - a closing, and
   - a signature.

☐ My sentences end with a period, an exclamation point, or a question mark.

☐ My sentences begin with capital letters.

PERSUASIVE LETTER

Planning Guide

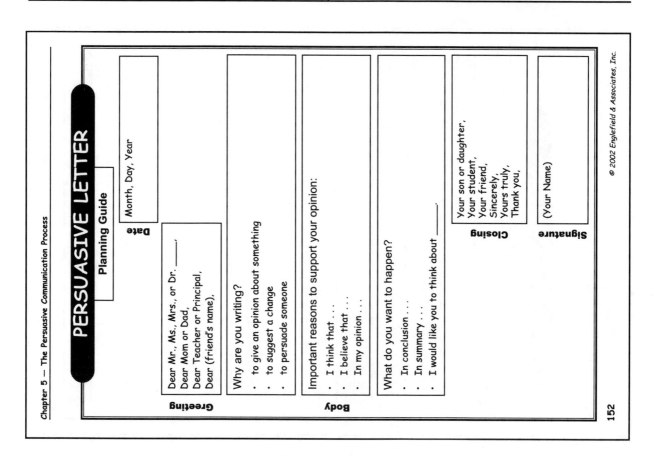

Date

Month, Day, Year

Greeting

Dear Mr., Ms., Mrs., or Dr. _____,
Dear Mom or Dad,
Dear Teacher or Principal,
Dear (friend's name),

Body

Why are you writing?
- to give an opinion about something
- to suggest a change
- to persuade someone

Important reasons to support your opinion:
- I think that . . . .
- I believe that . . . .
- In my opinion . . . .

What do you want to happen?
- In conclusion . . . .
- In summary . . . .
- I would like you to think about _____.

Closing

Your son or daughter,
Your student,
Your friend,
Sincerely,
Yours truly,
Thank you,

Signature

(Your Name)

152

Step

2

Remember, a good persuasive letter has the following parts.
- a date, a greeting, a body, a closing, and a signature
- a statement of your opinion
- facts that support your opinion
- a conclusion that restates your opinion

Step

3

Use the following idea to plan your persuasive letter.

Write a persuasive letter to your teacher. Persuade your teacher to let your class have extra time for recess.

Step

4

Use your planning guide and graphic organizer to help you think through your persuasive letter. You can use pictures or words to plan your persuasive letter.

151

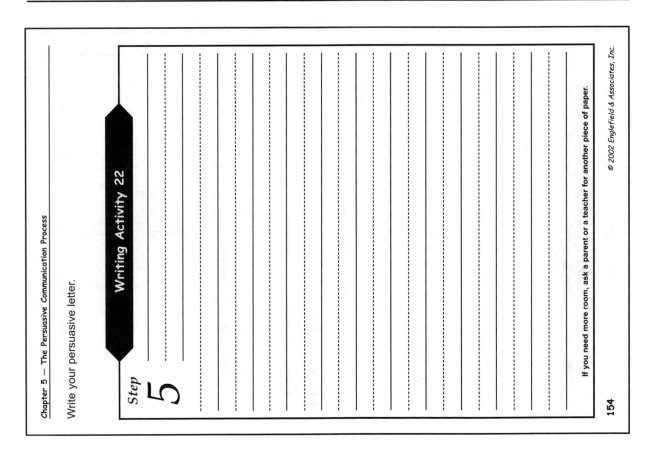

Chapter 5 — The Persuasive Communication Process

Write your persuasive letter.

Writing Activity 22

Step **5**

If you need more room, ask a parent or a teacher for another piece of paper.

154

© 2002 Englefield & Associates, Inc.

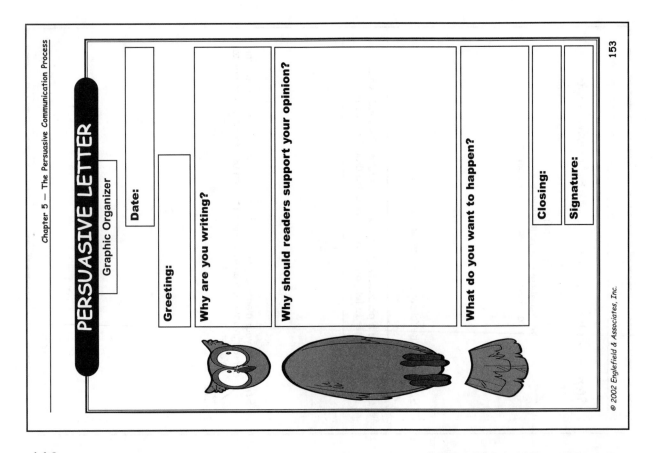

Chapter 5 — The Persuasive Communication Process

PERSUASIVE LETTER

Graphic Organizer

Date:

Greeting:

Why are you writing?

Why should readers support your opinion?

What do you want to happen?

Closing:

Signature:

153

© 2002 Englefield & Associates, Inc.

Step

6

The checklist shows what your best paper must have. Use the checklist below to review your work.

Checklist for Writing Activity 22

☐ I tell what I am writing my persuasive letter about.

☐ My letter gives reasons why I believe my opinion is important.

☐ In my conclusion, I say what I would like to happen.

☐ I use the form for a letter, including:
- a date,
- a greeting,
- a body,
- a closing, and
- a signature.

☐ My sentences end with a period, an exclamation point, or a question mark.

☐ My sentences begin with capital letters.

155

Additional Writing Prompts for Persuasion

1. Write a letter to your parents persuading them to let you stay up late.

2. Write a letter to your teacher about a classroom rule you would like to see changed. Persuade your teacher to change the rule.

3. You would like to go to a skating party. Persuade your parents to let you go to the skating party.

4. Persuade your friend to play a game with you.

5. Persuade your friend to come to your house to play.

6. Persuade your teacher to let your class have a party on Friday.

7. Persuade your parents to take you somewhere you like to go.

Additional Resources

The following titles will provide support for additional sources of models for each of the communication processes. You may want to utilize sections of the titles with your students to examine the features of the communication process as a reading or "read aloud" selection, or you may use an individual title in its entirety for classroom study. The model lesson from *Write on Target* can be paired with the appropriate graphic organizer and a model from the text for an easy-to-plan writing lesson. This list of titles is not meant to be complete; you can add to the list with materials from your own classroom.

Titles to Support the *Narrative Communication Process*

Ackerman, Karen	Song and Dance Man
Albee, Sarah	The Dragon's Scales
Brenner, Barbara	Beavers Beware!
Cowley, Joy	Agapanthus Hum and the Eyeglasses
Johnston, Tony	Sparky and Eddie: The First Day of School
Orgel, Doris	Button Soup
Wyeth, Sharon Dennis	Tomboy Trouble

Titles to Support the *Descriptive Communication Process*

Brighton, Catherine	Dearest Grandmama
Cazet, Denys	Minnie and Moo Save the Earth
Hautzig, Deborah	A Little Princess
Keats, Ezra Jack	A Letter to Amy
Schwartz, Alvin	In a Dark, Dark Room and Other Scary Stories

Titles to Support the *Direction Communication Process*

Miller, J.P. (illustrator)	The Little Red Hen: A Favorite Folk-Tale
Schade, Susan	Baseball Camp on the Planet of the Eyeballs

Titles to Support the *Explanation Communication Process*

Adler, David A.	Young Cam Jansen and the Missing Cookie
Dussling, Jennifer	Pink Snow and Other Weird Weather
Parish, Peggy	Amelia Bedelia
Sharmat, Marjorie Weinman	Nate the Great and Me: The Case of the Fleeing Fang

Titles to Support the *Persuasive Communication Process*

Giff, Patricia Reilly	Good Luck, Ronald Morgan!
Hooks, William H.	Mr. Monster
Morris, Kim	Molly in the Middle
Porte, Barbara Ann	Harry's Pony
Van Leeuwen, Jean	Amanda Pig, Schoolgirl